"The Contemporary Leader *is perfect for executives navigating today's complex business landscape. Tom Mawhinney delivers a powerful, actionable guide that blends timeless leadership principles with the modern skills necessary to succeed in an era of rapid change. His insights into professional, personal, and technological competencies provide a roadmap for leaders who want to drive innovation, foster resilience, and inspire teams. This book is a compelling and practical resource for those committed to evolving their leadership approach."*

—ERIK SEVERSEN, Bestselling Author of *Ordinary to Extraordinary*

"As a former Deloitte executive and Chief People Officer, I've read countless books on leadership and personal development, but The Contemporary Leader *stands out for its relevance and depth. Tom Mawhinney precisely identifies the challenges that today's leaders face. And he doesn't stop there—he provides a comprehensive framework to assess, develop, and apply the skills necessary for long-term success. This book is a must-read for any leader who wants to navigate the ever-evolving landscape of the future of work with confidence."*

—DARIA RUDNIK, Team Architect and Strategic Clarity Coach, Aidra.AI Founder and CEO

"With The Contemporary Leader, *Tom Mawhinney has built us all a mirror. If we're the least bit curious (see chapter 4), we'll grab the mirror with both hands and start asking questions. Bottom line: to what extent do our personal, professional, and technology skills reflect the needs of this contemporary business environment? And let's be honest with our answers, particularly when it comes to two terms that stood out to me: Translation and Technology Objectivity. Ignore at our peril."*

—GILES ATKINSON, Owner, Keystone Communications

"The business landscape is evolving and becoming more complex, with no sign of this complexity diminishing. These realities demand that leaders reflect on their strengths and develop their skills. Through The Contemporary Leader, *Tom Mawhinney delivers a practical field guide for leaders at all levels, equipping them with the essential competencies required to navigate uncertainty. With a blend of real-world examples, actionable insights, and a tactical approach to leadership development, this book serves as a playbook—helping leaders not just respond to complexity but harness it as a catalyst for personal and organizational growth."*

—JONNY STEVENS, Founder, Growth Champions Consulting

THE
CONTEMPORARY
LEADER

THE
CONTEMPORARY
LEADER

The Modern Skills Required to Lead, Adapt,
and Succeed in Today's Marketplace

TOM MAWHINNEY

THIN LEAF PRESS

Publication Data
Names: Mawhinney, Tom, Author
Titles: *The Contemporary Leader*

ISBN: 978-1-953183-76-7 (paperback) | 978-1-953183-75-0 (eBook)

Business, Money, Management, Leadership
Editors: Kristin Kaye, Dhanliza Cellona
Thin Leaf Press
Los Angeles

Book Cover Design and Interior Formatting by 100Covers.

THIN
LEAF

TABLE OF CONTENTS

INTRODUCTION

The Contemporary Leader In A Transformative World

Leadership has always been the cornerstone of organizational success. But in today's fast-paced and unpredictable business environment, its significance has grown exponentially. Contemporary leaders influence not just growth but also the performance, adaptability, and resilience of their organizations. As technology disrupts traditional models and societal expectations evolve, leaders are called upon to bridge strategy, innovation, and culture. This book, *The Contemporary Leader: The Modern Skills Required to Lead, Adapt, and Succeed in Today's Marketplace*, explores how leaders can meet these challenges head-on while seizing unprecedented opportunities.

The Purpose Behind This Book

Throughout my career as a board member, executive, and entrepreneur, I've observed how effective leadership can act as a catalyst for sustained growth and success. Conversely, I've seen how a lack of strong leadership can stifle progress, derail promising initiatives, and even jeopardize an organization's future. These experiences have solidified my belief that contemporary leadership skills are not merely "nice-to-have" attributes—they are essential drivers of organizational success in today's ever-evolving business climate.

The modern business environment demands a new breed of leader: one capable of navigating the complexities of hypercompetitive markets, embracing emerging technologies, and inspiring diverse, multi-generational teams. This book is a guide for those leaders—executives, board members, entrepreneurs, and aspiring leaders—who understand the need to evolve their skills to meet the demands of a dynamic and fast-changing world.

My motivation for writing this book is straightforward: to bridge the gap between the skills leaders have traditionally relied on and the competencies they must master to excel today. By equipping leaders with the insights and tools necessary to succeed, I aim to contribute to the growth and long-term success of organizations around the world.

The Rising Imperative Of Leadership In Modern Times

Leadership has long been the driving force behind success, but the demands placed on leaders today have evolved dramatically. In an era of rapid technological change, shifting workforce dynamics, and increasing market complexity, leadership is no longer just about managing operations—it's about driving strategy, fostering innovation, and building resilience within organizations.

Today's leaders face heightened expectations to navigate ambiguity, anticipate change, and deliver results in hypercompetitive environments. Beyond ensuring stability, leaders are tasked with charting paths for growth, inspiring teams, and creating conditions where innovation can thrive. This expanded mandate elevates leadership from a critical function to an indispensable foundation of organizational performance.

What sets contemporary leadership apart is the ability to bridge the gap between legacy practices and modern demands. Leaders must combine strategic foresight with the agility to adapt plans in real time, ensuring their organizations remain competitive in dynamic markets. Their decisions have a cascading impact across teams, operations, and outcomes, making the quality of leadership the defining factor in organizational performance.

The interconnected nature of today's business landscape amplifies the influence of leadership. Decisions made at the top affect everything from team alignment to market positioning, highlighting the need for leaders who can integrate vision, adaptability, and execution. This book is dedicated to equipping leaders with the skills required to meet these demands and to thrive amid the complexities of modern business. By embracing leadership excellence, organizations can not only navigate disruption but also turn it into an engine for growth and long-term success.

What You'll Find In This Book

This book is a practical guide for leaders navigating today's dynamic business environment, providing actionable strategies to drive innovation, foster resilience, and make a lasting impact.

- *Chapter 1—The Evolution of Leadership: Thriving in the Modern Business Environment*
  Explore the forces reshaping leadership and why today's leaders must evolve to succeed.

- *Chapter 2—Essential Skills for the Contemporary Leader: Professional, Personal, and Technology Competencies*
  Learn about the key domains and 15 essential skills that form the foundation of leadership in a complex world.

- *Chapter 3—Professional Skills: Building the Foundation for Leadership Excellence*
  Explore key professional competencies that drive organizational success.

- *Chapter 4—Personal Skills: The Traits That Transform Leaders*
  Discover how personal traits like adaptability and emotional intelligence (EI) can enhance leadership effectiveness.

- *Chapter 5—Technology Skills: Leading in a Digital and Data-driven World*

Understand the critical technology skills leaders need to embrace the digital age.

- *Chapter 6—Assessing and Developing Leadership Skills: A Revised Approach for a Changing World*
  Learn how to assess and develop leadership skills to meet the demands of today's evolving workplace.

- *Chapter 7—Leadership Deficiencies: The Cost of Neglecting Development*
  Examine how leadership gaps can undermine success and gain insights to address them.

- *Chapter 8—Leadership Development as the Ultimate Strategy: Making the Case for Long-term Success*
  Discover why leadership development is the most important strategy for long-term organizational success.

By the end of this book, you will understand what it takes to be a contemporary leader and how to apply these skills to make meaningful, lasting contributions to your organization and your career.

Why This Book Is Different

This book bridges the gap between timeless leadership principles and the essential skills required to navigate today's fast-changing business environment. While many leadership texts focus exclusively on traditional models or emerging trends, *The Contemporary Leader* integrates both into a practical framework. By addressing the three critical domains—professional, personal, and technology skills—this book equips leaders to recognize and respond to the unique demands of a modern marketplace.

Unlike other texts that rely heavily on theory or abstract case studies, this book prioritizes actionable insights and relatable examples. From well-documented success stories to recognizable challenges, the content is grounded in real-world contexts that resonate with leaders at all levels. The emphasis on skill identification and intentional development ensures readers leave with strategies they can immediately apply.

Whether you're a seasoned executive, an aspiring leader, or someone preparing for a significant career pivot, this book meets you where you are. Its unique value lies in highlighting the urgency of adapting to today's challenges while providing a clear pathway to develop the skills that matter most. *The Contemporary Leader* is not just about understanding leadership—it's about preparing yourself to lead effectively in an era of constant change and complexity.

By spotlighting the essential skills for success and the necessity of continuous development, this book empowers leaders to navigate today's challenges with confidence. The stakes for leadership have never been higher, and understanding these stakes is critical to staying relevant and impactful.

The Stakes For Leaders Today

The stakes for contemporary leaders extend beyond organizational performance metrics. In today's interconnected world, leadership defines not only a company's ability to sustain its competitive edge, retain talent, and innovate at scale but also the trajectory of an individual leader's career and influence. The evolving demands of leadership require individuals to continuously grow their capabilities to remain relevant, impactful, and fulfilled in their roles.

For the proactive leader, the ever-changing landscape is both a challenge and an opportunity. Evolving leadership skills like visioning, adaptability, and emotional intelligence can position you as a trusted problem solver, an inspiring innovator, and a sought-after leader in your industry. These skills are not just tools for navigating organizational complexity—they are essential for unlocking new opportunities in your career. Leaders who develop these increasingly critical skills can anticipate future trends, create compelling strategies, and inspire their teams to achieve ambitious goals.

Failure to adapt, on the other hand, can have profound consequences. Leaders who resist change risk becoming obsolete in a world that values agility and innovation. For organizations, this stagnation can lead to missed opportunities, low morale, and diminished competitiveness. For individuals, it can mean stalled career progression, reduced influence, and waning professional relevance.

Organizations that succeed in this environment will be those led by individuals who are proactive, adaptable, and deeply committed to continuous growth. These leaders will embrace change as an opportunity rather than a threat. They will view growth not as a checkbox but as a holistic process that extends beyond financial metrics to include personal development, cultural evolution, and operational excellence.

By evolving your leadership skills—including your capacity for visioning, cultivating emotional intelligence, and fostering adaptability—you invest not only in the success of your organization but also in your own capacity to thrive and lead in an ever-changing world. The journey toward becoming a contemporary leader is one of self-discovery, growth, and impact—one that leaves both individuals and organizations better prepared for the future.

A Call To Action

As you engage with this book, I encourage you to critically assess your leadership journey. What are the skills you excel in today, and where might you need to evolve? The business landscape is shifting at an unprecedented pace, requiring leaders to bridge legacy strengths with the demands of a modern, complex environment. Identifying your strengths and gaps is the first step in aligning your leadership capabilities with your organization's needs and future growth objectives.

This book provides a framework to help you take that step. By recognizing the essential skills outlined in these pages—whether professional, personal, or technological—you'll gain clarity on what it takes to remain relevant and effective. Consider this book not as an endpoint, but as a starting point for your ongoing growth as a leader. Reflect on the insights shared, challenge yourself to adopt new perspectives, and take action toward cultivating the skills necessary to thrive in a dynamic business world.

Leadership is not a fixed attribute—it's a journey of learning, adaptation, and intentional growth. My hope is that the lessons in this book inspire you to embrace this journey with purpose and determination. By committing to developing your leadership skills, you're not only ensuring your own growth but also creating a ripple effect that impacts your team, your organization, and the broader business environment. Let's take that journey together.

CHAPTER 1

THE EVOLUTION OF LEADERSHIP: THRIVING IN THE MODERN BUSINESS ENVIRONMENT

Leadership today is undergoing a seismic transformation. The strategies and traits that once defined effective leadership are no longer adequate to meet the demands of a complex and rapidly changing world. Leaders face unprecedented challenges: balancing traditional responsibilities such as decision making and strategy execution, with the agility to adapt to technological innovation, cultural shifts, and organizational disruption.

This chapter explores the driving forces behind these changes—the transformation of the business landscape, shifting employee expectations, and the growing impact of technology. These forces demand a new, multidimensional approach to leadership. To succeed, contemporary leaders must integrate professional expertise with personal authenticity and technological fluency, enabling them to navigate ambiguity and inspire others.

The need for leadership evolution is not optional—it is imperative. Organizations that fail to invest in leadership growth risk stagnation and irrelevance. Conversely, those that cultivate adaptable, forward-thinking leaders are poised to thrive amid uncertainty. This chapter illustrates the critical need for leaders to adapt by drawing on real-world examples and insights that lay the foundation for the skills discussed in subsequent chapters.

The Contemporary Leadership Imperative: Adapting To A Transforming Business Landscape

The modern business environment is defined by its volatility and interconnectedness. Globalization, once heralded as a pathway to boundless opportunity, now adds layers of complexity as international markets face geopolitical instability, shifting trade agreements, and cultural differences. Leaders must navigate an environment where local decisions can trigger global consequences, and supply chains are vulnerable to external shocks.

Industries are also facing relentless disruption from lean, innovative startups. These nimble competitors challenge established organizations to stay relevant by fostering cultures of agility and creativity. Leaders must adopt a mindset of continuous innovation and develop the foresight to anticipate new threats.

Moreover, the pace of change has accelerated to such a degree that long-term strategic planning has become a daunting challenge. Leaders must reevaluate their approach to strategy, developing resilience and agility to recalibrate plans on shorter timelines. The ability to manage ambiguity and lead teams with confidence is now essential for organizational success.

Practical Example: Facing the Uncertainty of Market Disruption
Amara, the chief executive officer (CEO) of a regional logistics company, faced mounting challenges as nimble competitors with tech-enabled delivery systems entered her market. Despite her company's strong

reputation, customer expectations for speed and transparency were rapidly evolving, and Amara found her organization struggling to adapt.

Confronted with shrinking market share and rising operational pressures, Amara recognized the urgent need to rethink her approach. The challenge was clear: Traditional methods that had driven past success were no longer sufficient in a landscape defined by disruption and complexity.

The Contemporary Leadership Imperative: Responding To Evolving Employee Expectations

Employees today have fundamentally different expectations of their leaders and organizations. Unlike previous generations, which prioritized job security and stability, modern employees seek roles that provide purpose, flexibility, and inclusivity. These shifts are transforming workplace dynamics and forcing leaders to adapt their approaches.

Flexibility is now a cornerstone of workforce demands. Remote and hybrid work arrangements, accelerated by the pandemic, have permanently altered how organizations operate. Leaders must balance the benefits of flexibility with the need to maintain productivity and cohesion, often requiring new technologies and reimagined workflows.

Inclusivity and mental well-being are also critical priorities. Employees increasingly expect their organizations to champion diversity, equity, and inclusion while fostering environments that support emotional health. Leadership today must center on authenticity, empathy, and the ability to empower individuals.

Practical Example: Struggling to Engage a Diverse Workforce

Kara, a senior leader at a global technology firm, faced growing challenges as her team expanded across multiple time zones and cultural contexts. Employees reported feeling disconnected, particularly in a remote work environment where opportunities for organic interactions were limited.

Simultaneously, Kara encountered growing tension around work-life balance, with employees calling for more autonomy in managing their schedules. Struggling to align these diverse needs with organizational goals, Kara found herself confronting a leadership challenge that demanded a new approach.

The Contemporary Leadership Imperative: Harnessing Technology's Transformative Power

Technology is a driving force of change, redefining industries and creating both opportunities and challenges. From artificial intelligence (AI) and machine learning to blockchain and IoT, these advancements promise unprecedented efficiency and innovation. However, leaders must navigate a host of complexities to successfully integrate new technologies into their organizations.

One major challenge is bridging the gap between innovation and strategy. Leaders must ensure that technology investments align with organizational goals and deliver measurable value. This requires a clear understanding of emerging technologies and their potential applications, as well as the foresight to anticipate risks.

Additionally, leaders must address the human implications of technology adoption. Automation, for instance, raises concerns about job security, while digital tools can expose skill gaps among employees. Leaders must approach these challenges with empathy, creating an environment where technology is seen as an enabler rather than a threat.

Practical Example: Struggling to Integrate Emerging Technologies

Marcus, the chief operating officer (COO) of a traditional retail chain, faced mounting pressure as e-commerce competitors leveraged AI-driven systems to revolutionize the customer experience. Recognizing the potential of similar technology, Marcus initiated discussions about digital transformation but found his organization unprepared for implementation.

Compounding the challenge, employees expressed resistance to automation tools, fearing job displacement. Marcus had to confront not just technical hurdles but also the cultural and ethical considerations of introducing transformative technologies.

Bridging The Gap: Why Leadership Must Evolve

The challenges outlined in the first half of this chapter—an ever-changing business landscape, evolving employee expectations, and the transformative impact of technology—underscore a pressing reality: The traditional approaches to leadership are no longer sufficient. Navigating these shifts requires more than an awareness of the changes; it demands a commitment to evolving leadership practices in alignment with these new realities.

As the world becomes increasingly dynamic and complex, the role of the leader must also transform. Today's leaders must cultivate new approaches that go beyond maintaining stability—they must inspire, innovate, and empower their teams to thrive in the face of uncertainty. This evolution is not about abandoning foundational leadership principles but rather adapting and expanding them to address contemporary demands.

In the next three subsections, this chapter will explore how leadership must adapt in response to the key challenges previously outlined. By examining the same scenarios presented earlier, we'll see how leaders like Amara, Kara, and Marcus evolved their leadership strategies to tackle disruption, foster engagement, and embrace innovation. These examples illustrate not only the "why" but also the "how" of leadership evolution, offering insights into what it takes to lead effectively in today's transformative world.

Adapting Leadership To A Transforming Business Landscape

To thrive in today's evolving business landscape, leaders must embrace strategies that prioritize agility, resilience, and proactive problem solving. The complexities of globalization, market disruptions, and shifting consumer expectations require leaders to look beyond traditional, hierarchical decision-making structures. Instead, they must empower their teams to act independently and collaborate effectively, fostering a culture of continuous adaptation and innovation.

Building resilience into organizational operations is another critical priority. Leaders must identify vulnerabilities in their supply chains, operational frameworks, and market strategies, implementing solutions that mitigate risks. Diversifying supply chains, forging strategic partnerships, and leveraging technology for predictive analysis are key tactics that allow organizations to anticipate disruptions and respond proactively. Resilience is no longer a "nice-to-have" quality—it is essential for navigating a landscape where volatility has become the norm.

Equally important is the need to balance short-term agility with long-term strategic planning. While rapid pivots may address immediate challenges, sustainable success requires leaders to maintain a clear vision and align their teams around shared objectives. By integrating resilience and agility into their leadership approach, contemporary leaders can transform the unpredictability of the modern business landscape into opportunities for growth and innovation.

Practical Example: Amara's Strategy to Navigate Complexity

Building on the challenges described earlier, Amara recognized that her company's reliance on a single supply chain model left it vulnerable to external shocks. She spearheaded a diversification strategy, establishing production hubs across multiple regions to reduce reliance on any single market. This decentralized model not only mitigated geopolitical risks but also allowed her organization to respond more flexibly to local market demands.

Amara also assembled cross-functional task forces to monitor emerging risks and identify strategic opportunities. These teams collaborated on contingency plans that could be quickly implemented in the event of supply chain disruptions. By fostering a culture of shared ownership and adaptability, Amara transformed her organization from a reactive entity into a proactive market leader, demonstrating the critical role of agility and foresight in addressing the challenges of the modern business environment.

Adapting Leadership To Evolving Employee Expectations

Addressing the shifting expectations of today's workforce requires leaders to cultivate environments that emphasize purpose, flexibility, and inclusivity. Employees increasingly prioritize roles that align with their personal values and provide opportunities for growth and fulfillment. Leaders who fail to recognize and respond to these changing dynamics risk disengagement, turnover, and diminished organizational performance.

Flexibility is integral to modern leadership. Remote and hybrid work arrangements have fundamentally redefined how teams collaborate and communicate, requiring leaders to implement systems that promote accountability while respecting individual autonomy. Leaders who embrace this shift and leverage technology to foster connection and collaboration can create environments where employees feel empowered to excel.

Inclusivity and emotional well-being are equally essential. Employees expect their leaders to champion diversity, equity, and inclusion, ensuring that all voices are heard and valued. This requires leaders to engage authentically, model empathy, and foster a culture where individuals feel safe to contribute their ideas and perspectives. By addressing these needs, leaders can build a resilient, motivated workforce capable of driving organizational success.

Practical Example: Kara's Approach to Rebuilding Culture

Returning to the challenges she faced, Kara knew that her organization's cultural issues required immediate and sustained attention. She launched a series of listening sessions to gather direct feedback from employees about their experiences and priorities. These discussions highlighted a need for greater inclusivity, mentorship opportunities, and flexibility in managing work-life balance.

In response, Kara implemented several initiatives, including structured mentorship programs that paired senior leaders with employees across departments, fostering professional growth and connection. She also introduced flexible scheduling policies and invested in diversity and inclusion training to address systemic issues within the organization. Over time, these efforts significantly improved employee engagement and retention, reinforcing the value of a leadership approach centered on empathy and inclusivity.

Adapting Leadership To Leverage Technology's Transformative Power

Harnessing the full potential of technology requires leaders to move beyond the technical aspects of implementation. Successful technology adoption hinges on aligning innovation with organizational strategy, fostering a culture of experimentation, and addressing the human dimensions of change. Leaders must act as both visionaries and facilitators, ensuring that technology serves as a tool for progress rather than a source of disruption.

Developing technological fluency is an essential component of this process. While leaders do not need to be experts in every emerging technology, they must understand enough to ask the right questions, evaluate potential opportunities, and guide their organizations toward impactful adoption. By fostering a collaborative approach, leaders can bridge the gap between innovation and execution, ensuring that technology investments deliver measurable value.

Addressing employee concerns about technology adoption is equally critical. Leaders must communicate transparently about the rationale behind technological changes, emphasizing how these tools enhance, rather than replace, human contributions. Providing comprehensive training and creating opportunities for employees to upskill can help alleviate fears and build confidence, fostering a culture where technology is embraced as a catalyst for growth.

Practical Example: Marcus's Digital Transformation Leadership

Building on the earlier challenges he faced, Marcus recognized that a successful digital transformation required more than simply adopting new tools. He began by forming a cross-functional team of technology advocates who worked to identify high-impact solutions, such as AI-driven inventory management and customer engagement systems. This team collaborated with external consultants to ensure a seamless integration process.

To address employee resistance, Marcus prioritized open communication, holding regular town halls to explain the benefits of the transformation and address concerns about automation. He also introduced targeted training programs to upskill employees, ensuring they could thrive in a technology-driven environment. These efforts not only improved operational efficiency but also fostered a sense of empowerment among employees, positioning the organization as a leader in its industry.

Chapter Summary

Leadership in the modern era is defined by transformation. The evolving business landscape, shifting employee expectations, and rapid technological advancements require leaders to adapt their approaches and skill sets to thrive in a complex environment. This chapter explored these driving forces, illustrating the challenges leaders face and the necessity for a multidimensional approach to leadership.

Through the journeys of Amara, Kara, and Marcus, the chapter demonstrated the practical realities of these challenges. Amara addressed global supply chain vulnerabilities by fostering collaboration and building resilience into her operations. Kara navigated the complexities of employee engagement by creating an inclusive, flexible culture. Marcus tackled the integration of transformative technologies by aligning innovation with strategy and empowering his workforce. Their stories underscore the importance of adaptability, empathy, and strategic foresight in navigating change and seizing opportunities.

Looking ahead, this chapter sets the stage for understanding the essential skills contemporary leaders need to address these challenges. By evolving their leadership practices, today's leaders can turn disruption into opportunity and position their organizations for sustained success in a fast-changing world.

CHAPTER 2

ESSENTIAL SKILLS FOR THE CONTEMPORARY LEADER: PROFESSIONAL, PERSONAL, AND TECHNOLOGY COMPETENCIES

Leadership in today's business landscape is a multidimensional challenge. To meet the demands of a fast-changing world, leaders must master a combination of traditional and emerging competencies that equip them to adapt, inspire, and innovate. This chapter introduces the 15 essential contemporary leadership skills, grouped into three interconnected domains: professional skills, personal skills, and technology skills. Together, these skills form a holistic framework for leadership excellence, addressing the complexities of modern organizations and workforce dynamics.

Professional skills provide the structural backbone for leadership, encompassing competencies such as visioning, decision making, and communication. Personal skills bring the human element to leadership, enabling trust, adaptability, and emotional intelligence. Technology skills reflect the growing importance of digital fluency, empowering leaders to embrace and leverage innovation effectively. This chapter highlights the interplay between these domains, illustrating how they collectively enable leaders to meet challenges and seize opportunities with confidence.

With practical examples and actionable insights, this chapter sets the stage for understanding how these 15 skills work in harmony to create balanced, impactful leadership. Each domain plays a vital role in equipping leaders to succeed in an era defined by rapid disruption, diverse teams, and relentless innovation.

Traditional Leadership Skills Remain Relevant

While the demands on leaders have evolved, foundational leadership skills remain indispensable. Core competencies like visioning, decision making, and communication have always been the backbone of effective leadership. These "table stakes" skills serve as the baseline for navigating complexity and enabling progress in any organizational context.

In the modern era, these foundational skills are more critical than ever. The increasing pace of change and rising complexity mean that clear vision, sound decision making, and transparent communication are essential to keeping teams aligned and engaged. Without these abilities, even the most innovative organizations risk losing momentum and direction.

Stakeholders—employees, customers, and investors alike—expect leaders to exhibit these skills with precision. The ability to articulate a clear vision builds trust and motivates teams, while strong communication fosters collaboration across diverse groups. Professional skills remain the structural backbone of leadership, ensuring that contemporary leaders can navigate ambiguity and drive results.

Practical Example: The Importance of Visioning and Communication

Alan, a technical expert recently promoted to a divisional leadership role, struggled with the transition. Despite his deep subject-matter expertise, he found it difficult to articulate a compelling vision for his team.

This lack of direction led to confusion, reduced morale, and misaligned efforts. Team members expressed frustration, unsure of how their work contributed to broader objectives.

Recognizing the need for improvement, Alan sought mentorship and training in visioning and communication. Over time, he learned to craft clear, inspiring messages that connected individual tasks to organizational goals. By improving his communication and providing a strong sense of purpose, Alan reinvigorated his team, increasing both engagement and performance.

Expanding Leadership Skills For A New Era

In addition to foundational competencies, leaders now face heightened expectations to excel in two additional domains: personal skills and technology skills. These skills are no longer optional—they are vital for navigating today's dynamic business environment.

Personal skills, such as emotional intelligence, resilience, and adaptability, allow leaders to build trust, manage diverse teams, and navigate challenges with composure. As organizations grow more diverse and workforce dynamics evolve, these skills are essential for creating environments where employees feel empowered and included.

Technology skills have also become a defining aspect of modern leadership. The ability to leverage AI, data analytics, and other innovations is now a key differentiator, enabling leaders to drive strategic decisions and operational efficiency. By integrating these domains, leaders create a multidimensional profile capable of thriving amid disruption and change.

Practical Example: Expanding Leadership Competencies for Impact

Sarah, the COO of a global manufacturing company, had always excelled in traditional leadership skills but struggled to connect with her team on a personal level. Her lack of emotional intelligence created barriers—particularly when managing cross-cultural teams—and her limited technological literacy hindered the company's digital transformation efforts.

Determined to grow, Sarah invested in professional development focused on emotional intelligence and technological fluency. She began engaging her teams with empathy, fostering stronger collaboration and trust. Simultaneously, she upskilled in data analytics to lead the company's digital initiatives more effectively. These efforts resulted in increased employee engagement, operational improvements, and greater alignment with the organization's strategic goals.

The Interdependence Of Contemporary Leadership Skills

Contemporary leadership requires a diverse set of skills that work in tandem to address the complexities of modern business. These skills are not isolated; instead, they are deeply interconnected, with mastery in one often enhancing the effectiveness of others. Together, they create a synergistic effect that strengthens overall leadership impact.

For example, strong visioning provides strategic clarity, but without effective communication, even the most compelling vision may fail to resonate. Similarly, emotional intelligence enhances collaboration, while technological fluency adds depth to decision making. Leaders who develop a balanced skillset across these dimensions are better equipped to navigate complex challenges and seize opportunities.

This interconnectedness underscores the importance of cultivating a holistic leadership profile. By integrating a range of professional, personal, and technological competencies, leaders can address the multifaceted demands of modern organizations and create environments that foster innovation, trust, and growth.

Practical Example: Achieving Synergy Through Holistic Leadership

Emma, the CEO of a regional energy company, recognized the need for a holistic skillset to lead her organization through a period of regulatory changes and industry disruption. She focused on developing technological fluency to spearhead digital transformation efforts while simultaneously improving her emotional intelligence to build stronger relationships with her executive team.

These efforts paid off when Emma led a successful initiative to integrate AI into the company's energy efficiency programs. Her technological awareness enabled her to identify the right tools, while her resilience and communication skills helped her navigate regulatory hurdles and inspire her team. This comprehensive approach positioned her company as an industry leader, demonstrating the power of interconnected leadership skills.

Transitioning To Chapters 3–5: Introducing The Leadership Domains

The 15 essential contemporary leadership skills presented in this chapter are grouped into three core domains: professional skills, personal skills, and technology skills. Each domain represents a vital aspect of contemporary leadership, addressing the challenges outlined earlier in the chapter—an evolving business landscape, shifting employee expectations, and the transformative power of technology. Together, these domains equip leaders to navigate complexity, foster innovation, and drive organizational growth.

Below is a summary of the skills within each domain, highlighting how they address the unique demands of today's environment. These domains are interconnected, and leaders who integrate competencies across them are better prepared to lead in a fast-changing world.

Professional Skills: Building The Foundation For Leadership Excellence

These are the traditional yet indispensable skills that provide structure and clarity to leadership. They allow leaders to establish direction, inspire teams, and align efforts toward shared goals, ensuring stability in a dynamic environment.

1. *Visioning*: Crafting a compelling, long-term direction that inspires confidence and guides decision making. In an unpredictable landscape, a clear vision helps teams stay focused and aligned.

2. *Translation*: Transforming strategic visions into actionable plans that align with organizational capabilities. Leaders must bridge the gap between strategy and execution to ensure progress.

3. *Problem Solving*: Addressing challenges methodically and creatively to remove barriers and advance objectives. This skill is critical in overcoming obstacles while maintaining momentum.

4. *Decision Making*: Making timely, impactful choices that balance risks with opportunities. In high-stakes scenarios, effective decision making ensures organizational agility.

5. *Communication*: Conveying ideas, strategies, and expectations with clarity and purpose to diverse audiences. Strong communication fosters trust and drives collaboration.

6. *Motivation*: Energizing teams to achieve goals and sustain engagement. By fostering a sense of purpose, leaders inspire performance and innovation.

These skills form the backbone of leadership, enabling leaders to guide their teams through uncertainty while maintaining focus on organizational objectives.

Personal Skills: The Traits That Transform Leaders

Human-centered skills define how leaders connect with others, build trust, and navigate adversity with grace. They are essential for fostering engagement, inclusivity, and collaboration in diverse and evolving workforces.

1. *Coaching:* Empowering others by supporting their development and growth through guidance and feedback. Leaders who invest in coaching foster a culture of continuous learning and improvement.

2. *Authenticity:* Leading with integrity by aligning actions with values and organizational missions. Authenticity builds trust and inspires loyalty in teams.

3. *Emotional Intelligence:* Understanding and managing your emotions while responding effectively to those of others. This skill is critical for fostering collaboration and resolving conflicts.

4. *Curiosity:* Staying open to new ideas, seeking out learning opportunities, and fostering innovation. Curiosity drives creativity and helps leaders adapt to change.

5. *Adaptability:* Adjusting strategies and behaviors in response to evolving circumstances and challenges. Leaders must remain flexible to lead effectively through disruption.

6. *Resilience:* Recovering quickly from setbacks and maintaining focus on long-term success. Resilience enables leaders to inspire confidence even in difficult times.

These skills emphasize the human element of leadership, enabling leaders to build strong, trusting relationships while navigating the complexities of modern organizations.

Technology Skills: Leading In A Digital And Data-Driven World

In today's rapidly evolving digital landscape, technology literacy empowers leaders to harness innovation strategically and effectively. These skills bridge the gap between technical advancements and organizational goals.

1. *Technology Awareness:* Staying informed about emerging technologies and understanding their potential impact. Awareness helps leaders identify opportunities and anticipate challenges.

2. *Technology Objectivity:* Evaluating technology solutions without bias to ensure alignment with organizational goals. Leaders must balance innovation with practicality to drive value.

3. *Technology Application:* Translating technological possibilities into actionable initiatives that enhance efficiency and innovation. This skill enables leaders to integrate technology into their strategies seamlessly.

Technology skills are essential for leaders to remain competitive in a digital-first world, equipping them to lead with foresight and innovation.

A Comprehensive Skillset For Leadership Excellence

Together, these 15 essential skills form a robust framework for navigating the demands of modern leadership. Each domain contributes unique strengths to the overall leadership profile, and their integration enables leaders to address disruption, foster innovation, and inspire growth.

The chapters that follow will explore these domains in depth:

1. *Chapter 3—Professional Skills: Building the Foundation for Leadership Excellence*
   Learn how timeless skills like visioning, decision making, and communication remain essential and how to refine them for today's challenges.

2. *Chapter 4—Personal Skills: The Traits That Transform Leaders*
   Explore how emotional intelligence, adaptability, and resilience elevate leadership impact by building trust and inspiring teams.

3. *Chapter 5—Technology Skills: Leading in a Digital and Data-driven World*
Discover how technology awareness, objectivity, and application empower leaders to harness innovation and drive strategic advantage.

Chapter Summary

This chapter introduced the 15 essential leadership skills, grouped into the domains of professional skills, personal skills, and technology skills. These domains collectively address the challenges of contemporary leadership by combining structural expertise, relational depth, and technological acumen.

Professional skills, such as visioning and communication, provide the foundation for effective leadership by enabling clarity, direction, and alignment. Personal skills, including emotional intelligence and resilience, equip leaders to connect authentically with their teams and navigate challenges with empathy. Technology skills, like technology awareness and application, empower leaders to embrace digital innovation, making it a cornerstone of competitive advantage.

The interdependence of these skills underscores the need for a balanced approach. Leaders who cultivate competencies across all three domains can adapt to disruption, foster collaboration, and inspire innovation. As we move forward, the next chapters will provide a detailed exploration of these skills, beginning with professional skills in Chapter 3. By fully embracing these essential competencies, leaders can position themselves and their organizations for success in an ever-evolving business landscape.

CHAPTER 3

PROFESSIONAL SKILLS: BUILDING THE FOUNDATION FOR LEADERSHIP EXCELLENCE

Professional skills are the cornerstone of effective leadership, enabling leaders to set direction, align teams, and drive results. These time-tested competencies remain as relevant today as ever, even as the business landscape grows more dynamic and complex. This chapter focuses on six essential professional skills: visioning, translation, problem solving, decision making, communication, and motivation. Together, these skills provide the foundation for leaders to inspire confidence, execute strategies, and navigate challenges effectively.

In today's fast-paced environment, professional skills must be both timeless and adaptable. Leaders are expected to maintain clarity amidst uncertainty, make decisive choices under pressure, and motivate teams to achieve shared goals. This chapter examines how these skills are not only the backbone of leadership but also evolving to meet contemporary demands. Practical examples and actionable strategies provide insight into how these competencies empower leaders to navigate complexity and deliver impactful results.

Mastering professional skills is essential for achieving organizational alignment, driving innovation, and inspiring teams. By developing these core competencies, leaders can create a strong foundation upon which they can build the additional relational and technological capabilities that modern leadership requires.

The Core Of Effective Leadership

Professional skills form the critical link between strategy and execution, enabling leaders to navigate the demands of today's fast-paced and complex business environment. While personal skills strengthen relationships and technology skills drive innovation, professional skills are the foundation upon which all leadership competencies converge. They anchor leaders in clarity, focus, and purposeful action, providing stability even in uncertain times.

In the modern leadership landscape, these skills extend beyond traditional proficiency. It is no longer enough to simply articulate a vision or make sound decisions—leaders must inspire teams, foster alignment, and adapt strategies to dynamic circumstances. This blend of timeless expertise and modern agility defines the essence of effective leadership.

By mastering professional skills, leaders create the conditions for sustainable success. They enable organizations to thrive by aligning goals with execution, empowering teams, and integrating relational and technological capabilities into cohesive strategies. This foundational strength ensures leaders are not only prepared to respond to challenges but are also equipped to anticipate and shape the future.

Why Professional Skills Are Indispensable

Professional skills serve as the stabilizing force in an era of unpredictability. They anchor leaders in clarity and purpose, enabling them to:

1. *Articulate a Compelling Vision:* Leaders must craft and communicate a roadmap that inspires confidence and guides their organization forward.

2. *Turn Vision into Action:* A strong strategy is essential, but execution requires thoughtful translation of goals into actionable steps.

3. *Guide Decision Making Under Pressure:* Every choice has consequences. Leaders who can evaluate risks and opportunities with precision build trust and drive results.

4. *Build Confidence Through Communication:* Clear, effective communication ensures alignment and fosters collaboration across diverse teams.

5. *Inspire and Motivate Teams:* Beyond tasks and processes, professional skills ignite passion, creating an environment where employees feel empowered and engaged.

An Overview Of The Professional Skills

This chapter dives deep into the six essential professional skills that every contemporary leader must master:

1. *Visioning:* The ability to define and articulate a long-term strategic direction that motivates stakeholders and drives success.

2. *Translation:* Converting high-level aspirations into actionable strategies that align with organizational priorities and capabilities.

3. *Problem Solving:* Addressing challenges with analytical rigor and creative innovation to remove barriers and seize opportunities.

4. *Decision Making:* Making timely, high-impact decisions that balance risk and opportunity while ensuring alignment with broader objectives.

5. *Communication:* Delivering clear, purpose-driven messages to ensure alignment, understanding, and collaboration.

6. *Motivation:* Energizing teams by creating a shared sense of purpose and fostering engagement that sustains high performance.

Each of these skills builds on the others, creating a robust framework for leadership excellence. The ability to seamlessly integrate these competencies allows leaders to navigate complexity, inspire trust, and drive lasting results.

A Detailed Review Of The Professional Skills

In the following sections, we will examine each of these six professional skills in detail, beginning with visioning—the essential skill that enables leaders to define a compelling strategic direction for their teams and organizations.

ESSENTIAL LEADERSHIP SKILL #1: VISIONING

The Definition Of Visioning

Visioning is a leader's ability to craft a compelling and strategic path for their organization—one that not only ensures sustained success but also differentiates the organization in the marketplace. This skill involves imagining a future state that inspires stakeholders, aligns teams, and provides clarity about long-term goals and priorities. A strong vision acts as a North Star, guiding decision making, resource allocation, and organizational strategy while rallying employees, investors, and customers around a shared purpose.

Developing a vision is more than simply outlining business objectives—it requires leaders to think expansively about industry trends, societal shifts, and emerging opportunities. A well-crafted vision should resonate beyond the present moment, creating a roadmap that sustains momentum and keeps an organization focused amid rapid change.

The Vital Importance Of Visioning

Visioning is one of the most critical skills a leader can develop because it serves as the foundation upon which all other leadership actions are built. Without a clear and compelling vision, organizations risk stagnation, misalignment, and an inability to respond effectively to market changes. Leaders who master visioning are better equipped to inspire confidence, attract investment, and position their organizations for long-term success.

1. Strategic Direction and Differentiation

A strong vision provides a roadmap for achieving differentiated success. In today's highly competitive and rapidly evolving business environment, organizations cannot afford to pursue incremental growth alone. Visioning allows leaders to anticipate industry trends, identify unique opportunities, and craft bold strategies that set their organizations apart. A well-articulated vision ensures that all efforts are aligned, reducing wasted time and resources while sharpening competitive focus.

2. Inspiring and Mobilizing Teams

One of the hallmarks of effective visioning is the ability to inspire action. Employees who understand and believe in their organization's vision are more engaged, motivated, and aligned with strategic priorities. A compelling vision fosters a sense of shared purpose, which has been shown to improve employee satisfaction, retention, and productivity. Leaders who excel in visioning can turn even the most ambitious goals into rallying points for their teams, ensuring alignment across all levels of the organization.

3. Adapting to Change

In a world of constant disruption, visioning is not about predicting the future—it's about preparing for it. Effective visioning allows leaders to anticipate market shifts, emerging technologies, and evolving customer expectations. By envisioning multiple potential futures, leaders can position their organizations to adapt quickly, pivot effectively, and seize opportunities before competitors do.

4. Building Stakeholder Confidence

A compelling vision is critical for gaining buy-in from stakeholders, including investors, board members, and customers. Leaders who can articulate a clear path forward demonstrate strategic foresight and instill confidence in their ability to navigate uncertainty. This confidence is essential for securing resources, partnerships, and long-term loyalty in a competitive environment. A well-communicated vision reassures stakeholders that the organization is forward-thinking, innovative, and prepared to lead.

With a strong vision in place, leaders must ensure that it is clearly communicated and resonates with stakeholders. This requires integrating several key components of effective visioning.

Key Components Of Visioning

To master visioning, leaders must integrate several critical components:

- *Clarity:* A vision must be concise and easily understood by all stakeholders. Overly complex or ambiguous visions dilute impact and reduce engagement, making alignment difficult.

- *Inspiration:* The vision should resonate emotionally, giving stakeholders a compelling reason to believe in and rally around the organization's future. A vision without passion is unlikely to drive action.

- *Practicality:* While aspirational, a vision should also feel achievable. Leaders must balance ambition with realism to ensure that stakeholders remain engaged and confident in the path forward.

- *Alignment:* A vision is most powerful when it aligns with the organization's values, mission, and culture. Misalignment can lead to resistance and disengagement, making execution more difficult.

- *Differentiation:* A distinctive vision sets an organization apart from competitors. It is not enough for a vision to inspire and align—it must also define what makes the organization unique in the marketplace.

By integrating these key components, leaders ensure that their vision is compelling, actionable, and resilient in the face of change.

Familiar Examples Of Effective Visioning

Tesla: Accelerating the Transition to Sustainable Energy

Elon Musk's vision of accelerating the world's transition to sustainable energy has propelled Tesla from a niche car manufacturer to a global leader in electric vehicles (EV) and renewable energy solutions. This clear, inspiring vision shapes Tesla's product roadmap and galvanizes employees, investors, and customers alike.

Unilever's Sustainable Living Plan: Driving Purpose-driven Growth

Unilever's board of directors played a pivotal role in driving the company's vision for sustainable growth. By championing the Sustainable Living Plan, the board set ambitious goals to reduce environmental impact, improve health outcomes, and enhance livelihoods. This vision not only aligned with stakeholder expectations but also positioned Unilever as a global leader in corporate responsibility and long-term value creation.

Microsoft's Cloud-First Transformation

When Satya Nadella became CEO of Microsoft, he envisioned a shift from a traditional software company to a cloud-first, mobile-first organization. This vision realigned Microsoft's strategy, reinvigorated its innovation pipeline, and restored its position as a leader in the tech industry. Nadella's vision helped Microsoft move away from legacy thinking and embrace modern, cloud-based solutions that better serve today's businesses and consumers.

Each of these examples highlights how a bold, well-defined vision can transform organizations, inspire action, and drive long-term success.

Visioning As A Repeatable Skill

Visioning is an ongoing process that evolves alongside market dynamics, organizational priorities, and emerging opportunities. A strong vision must remain adaptable, ensuring it stays relevant while maintaining its core purpose. Leaders who regularly refine their vision help their organizations maintain long-term focus and agility in an ever-changing environment.

Sustaining an impactful vision requires active engagement with stakeholders. Involving employees, board members, customers, and partners in the visioning process builds collective ownership and alignment. A well-communicated vision unifies efforts, strengthens buy-in, and inspires ongoing commitment to shared goals, ensuring that all levels of the organization remain focused and motivated.

Leaders must also track progress against their vision to maintain alignment and momentum. Regularly assessing strategic initiatives, communicating milestones, and celebrating progress reinforces belief in the vision while allowing for necessary adjustments. By treating visioning as a dynamic, repeatable process, leaders ensure their organizations remain forward-thinking, resilient, and positioned for sustained success.

ESSENTIAL LEADERSHIP SKILL #2: TRANSLATION

The Definition Of Translation

Translation is a leader's ability to convert a compelling vision into a viable, actionable plan tailored to the organization's unique context. This skill bridges the gap between aspiration and execution by transforming high-level strategic goals into practical, tangible initiatives. Effective translation ensures that a vision is not only inspirational but also achievable, empowering teams to understand their roles in realizing organizational objectives.

Leaders who excel in translation provide clear direction, structure, and accountability. Without this skill, even the most compelling vision can remain an abstract concept rather than a driver of meaningful results.

The Vital Importance Of Translation

Translation is where strategy meets action, making it a critical skill for ensuring that visions do not remain lofty ideals but become drivers of real-world outcomes.

1. Bridging the Gap Between Vision and Execution

A powerful vision sets the destination, but translation provides the map. By breaking down ambitious goals into actionable steps, leaders ensure that their teams have clear paths forward. This ability reduces confusion, improves resource allocation, and accelerates progress.

2. Ensuring Relevance to the Organization

Translation tailors the vision to fit the organization's specific needs, resources, and constraints. Leaders must account for factors like industry dynamics, workforce capabilities, and competitive positioning when creating actionable plans.

3. Empowering Teams to Take Ownership

Leaders who excel in translation empower their teams by providing clarity on roles, responsibilities, and expectations. When employees understand how their contributions fit into the broader strategy, they are more engaged and motivated.

4. Building Momentum Through Early Wins

Translation helps leaders prioritize initiatives that deliver quick, tangible results. These early wins build confidence, reinforce belief in the vision, and encourage stakeholders to stay invested in the journey.

With a clear strategy in place, leaders must ensure that translation incorporates structured execution and ongoing alignment.

Key Components Of Translation

To master translation, leaders must integrate several critical components:

- *Clarity:* Break complex goals into straightforward steps, ensuring all team members understand their roles and how their actions contribute to the vision.

- *Prioritization:* Focus on the most impactful initiatives that align with organizational goals and resources to drive progress efficiently.

- *Alignment:* Tailor plans to fit the organization's culture, values, and capabilities, ensuring consistency and unity across teams.

- *Communication:* Clearly convey the strategy to inspire confidence and secure buy-in, emphasizing transparency and shared purpose.

- *Flexibility:* Build adaptability into plans to respond to changing conditions while staying aligned with overarching objectives.

By integrating these key components, leaders ensure that their vision is transformed into sustainable execution strategies.

Familiar Examples Of Effective Translation

Amazon's Operational Excellence

Jeff Bezos' vision for Amazon as "the Earth's most customer-centric company" was translated into specific initiatives, such as same-day delivery and one-click purchasing. These tangible actions became hallmarks of Amazon's operational strategy, enabling it to dominate the e-commerce market.

Walt Disney's Theme Parks

Walt Disney envisioned a place where families could "have fun together," and he translated that ideal into Disneyland—a meticulously designed park where every attraction, service, and employee experience reflected that vision.

LEGO's Strategic Revival

When LEGO faced financial difficulties, CEO Jørgen Vig Knudstorp translated the company's vision of "creative play" into a strategy that prioritized innovation in core product lines while cutting non-essential projects. This focus revived LEGO's profitability and reaffirmed its leadership in the toy industry.

Each of these examples illustrates how effective translation ensures that a vision does not remain an idea—it becomes a driver of real-world success.

Translation As A Repeatable Skill

Translation is an evolving practice that requires leaders to refine execution strategies as business conditions change. Even the most well-structured plans must be reassessed to ensure they remain relevant, actionable, and aligned with organizational goals. Leaders who balance strategic consistency with adaptability keep their teams focused while staying responsive to new challenges and opportunities.

Sustaining translation requires collaboration and feedback. Actively engaging employees, stakeholders, and industry insights helps refine strategies and improve execution. Encouraging cross-functional teamwork fosters alignment and agility, ensuring that organizations can adapt swiftly to unforeseen challenges. Transparent communication keeps contributors engaged and committed to delivering results.

Tracking progress and celebrating milestones help maintain momentum. Measuring success through key performance indicators (KPIs) and regularly evaluating execution effectiveness allow leaders to make necessary adjustments. By reinforcing commitment to the vision while staying flexible, leaders ensure that translation remains a dynamic and results-driven process that delivers meaningful impact.

ESSENTIAL LEADERSHIP SKILL #3: PROBLEM SOLVING

Definition Of Problem Solving

Problem solving is a leader's ability to analyze objective data and subjective input in parallel to identify, address, and resolve priority issues within an organization. This skill involves identifying root causes, evaluating potential solutions, and implementing strategies that effectively tackle challenges while minimizing risks.

Successful problem solving requires a balance of analytical thinking, creative innovation, and emotional intelligence, ensuring that solutions are both data-driven and contextually appropriate. Leaders who excel in problem solving can navigate complexity, remove barriers to progress, and foster innovation, making this skill indispensable in today's rapidly changing business landscape.

The Vital Importance Of Problem Solving

Problem solving is at the core of effective leadership. In a world characterized by uncertainty, complexity, and rapid change, leaders constantly face challenges that require thoughtful and decisive action. The ability to tackle these challenges directly impacts an organization's agility, resilience, and long-term success.

1. Driving Organizational Progress

Organizations encounter obstacles at every level, from operational inefficiencies to strategic misalignments. Effective problem solving removes these barriers, paving the way for progress and sustained growth. Leaders who address issues swiftly and effectively significantly accelerate an organization's trajectory toward its goals.

2. Building Confidence Among Stakeholders

Leaders who demonstrate strong problem-solving abilities inspire confidence in employees, customers, and investors. Stakeholders trust leaders who show that they can navigate uncertainty and resolve issues effectively, strengthening engagement, loyalty, and long-term support, even during challenging times.

3. Fostering Innovation

Problem solving is not just about fixing what's broken—it often involves thinking outside the box and encouraging leaders to explore unconventional solutions. This mindset not only resolves immediate challenges but also drives innovation, creating new opportunities for an organization to differentiate itself in the marketplace.

4. Promoting Collaboration

Effective problem solving requires leaders to gather diverse perspectives, blending data analysis with insights from key stakeholders. A collaborative approach ensures that solutions are comprehensive and take into account varied needs and insights. By involving teams in the problem-solving process, leaders build stronger relationships and enhance organizational cohesion.

With the right problem-solving strategies in place, leaders ensure that their organizations remain resilient, adaptable, and well-equipped to navigate challenges.

Key Components Of Problem Solving

To master problem solving, leaders must integrate several critical components:

- *Analytical Thinking*: Break challenges into components, use data to uncover root causes, and evaluate solutions based on evidence.

- *Creativity*: Explore innovative ideas and unconventional solutions to address issues effectively and stand out in competitive markets.

- *Decisiveness*: Act swiftly and confidently once the best course of action is identified, minimizing delays and uncertainty.

- *Emotional Intelligence*: Address the human side of challenges by considering the needs and perspectives of those affected.

- *Collaboration*: Involve diverse perspectives to create well-rounded solutions while fostering teamwork and unity.

By integrating these key components, leaders ensure that problems are addressed efficiently while fostering long-term innovation and growth.

Familiar Examples Of Effective Problem Solving

Johnson & Johnson's Tylenol Crisis

In the 1980s, Johnson & Johnson faced a major crisis when tampered Tylenol capsules led to consumer deaths. The company's leadership demonstrated exceptional problem-solving by recalling all products, prioritizing consumer safety, and introducing tamper-proof packaging. This response not only resolved the immediate issue but also restored consumer trust and set a new industry standard for safety.

Netflix's Pivot to Streaming

When Netflix's DVD rental model faced declining relevance, the company's leadership identified streaming technology as a solution to their problem of market saturation. By investing heavily in streaming, Netflix not only resolved its immediate challenges but also became a global leader in entertainment innovation.

Wells Fargo's Board Oversight During the Sales Scandal

Following revelations of fraudulent sales practices, Wells Fargo's board of directors took decisive steps to address the problem. They replaced key executives, implemented stricter oversight, and restructured governance practices to rebuild trust with customers and regulators. These actions demonstrated strategic problem solving in addressing systemic issues and preventing future misconduct.

Each of these examples highlights how strong problem-solving skills can turn crises into opportunities for trust-building and innovation.

Problem Solving As A Repeatable Skill

Effective leaders recognize that challenges are constant and that pro-actively addressing them ensures long-term resilience. By maintaining curiosity and adaptability, leaders keep problem solving a forward-looking function rather than a reactive response, allowing organizations to navigate complexity with agility.

Anticipating challenges is key to effective problem solving. Leaders who identify risks early can implement preventive measures, reducing disruptions and positioning their organizations for success. Staying attuned to industry trends, team dynamics, and external shifts enables leaders to make informed decisions and create contingency plans that enhance stability.

Embedding problem solving into an organization's culture ensures lasting impact. Leaders who facilitate open communication, encourage diverse perspectives, and promote a solutions-oriented mindset empower teams to tackle challenges collaboratively. By continuously refining problem-solving strategies and learning from past experiences, organizations become more innovative, adaptable, and prepared for long-term success.

ESSENTIAL LEADERSHIP SKILL #4: DECISION MAKING

Definition Of Decision Making

Decision making is the leader's ability to make impactful choices in a timely manner, enabling the organization to achieve its objectives. This skill involves evaluating options, considering both short-term and long-term implications, and balancing risk with opportunity.

Effective decision making requires clarity, confidence, and a deep understanding of organizational goals, ensuring that decisions are aligned with the broader vision and strategy. Leaders who master decision making provide direction, maintain momentum, and instill trust among stakeholders by demonstrating sound judgment and decisive action.

The Vital Importance Of Decision Making

In a rapidly changing business environment, decision making is a cornerstone of effective leadership. The ability to make sound decisions, often under pressure, directly impacts an organization's performance, adaptability, and long-term success. Leaders who excel in decision making drive progress, build trust, and create a foundation for sustained growth.

1. Maintaining Organizational Momentum

Timely decisions are essential for maintaining momentum within an organization. Delayed or indecisive actions can create bottlenecks, slow progress, and frustrate teams. Leaders who act decisively keep their organizations agile and responsive, ensuring that opportunities are seized, and challenges are addressed efficiently.

2. Balancing Risk and Reward

Every decision carries inherent risks, but great leaders have the ability to weigh those risks against potential rewards. Decision making is not about eliminating risk entirely—it's about managing it effectively while pursuing opportunities that align with organizational priorities. Leaders who strike this balance foster innovation and growth while safeguarding stability.

3. Empowering Teams Through Clarity

Decisive leadership provides clarity for teams, ensuring alignment around objectives and strategies. When leaders make impactful decisions and communicate them effectively, they empower their teams to execute with confidence and purpose. This clarity minimizes confusion and fosters a culture of accountability and trust.

4. Navigating Uncertainty

In periods of uncertainty, organizations look to their leaders for guidance. Decision making is critical during these times, as it reassures stakeholders and demonstrates the leader's ability to steer the organization through ambiguity. Leaders who excel in decision making help their teams stay focused and motivated, even in the face of significant challenges.

With a strong decision-making framework, leaders ensure that their organizations remain proactive, adaptable, and ready to seize new opportunities.

Key Components Of Decision Making

To master decision making, leaders must integrate several critical components:

- *Clarity of Purpose:* Align every decision with the organization's goals and vision, ensuring resources are directed toward meaningful priorities.

- *Information Gathering:* Use data and insights from diverse sources to evaluate options effectively without falling into analysis paralysis.

- *Risk Management:* Balance risks and opportunities by assessing potential outcomes and pursuing options that encourage innovation while minimizing downsides.

- *Decisiveness:* Act promptly and confidently based on available information to maintain momentum and avoid inefficiencies caused by prolonged deliberation.

- *Accountability:* Own the outcomes of decisions, fostering trust and creating a culture where teams feel empowered to act on shared goals.

By integrating these key components, leaders ensure that their decisions are well-informed, timely, and strategically aligned.

Familiar Examples Of Effective Decision Making

Apple's Decision to Focus on the iPhone

When Steve Jobs decided to pivot Apple's resources toward the development of the iPhone, it was a bold and high-stakes choice. This decision required reallocating efforts from other projects, but it ultimately revolutionized the technology industry and cemented Apple's position as a market leader.

Pfizer's Board Approval of the COVID-19 Vaccine Strategy

Pfizer's board of directors played a critical role in the decision to prioritize and fast-track the development of the COVID-19 vaccine. By allocating significant resources to this initiative and partnering with BioNTech, the board demonstrated decisive leadership, balancing urgency with safety. This decision not only addressed a global health crisis but also strengthened Pfizer's reputation for innovation and impact.

Ford's Decision to Focus on Electric Vehicles

Ford's recent shift to prioritize electric vehicles is a testament to decisive leadership responding to market and regulatory pressures. By committing significant resources to EV development, Ford has positioned itself as a forward-thinking player in the automotive industry.

Each of these examples highlights how strategic decision making can shape industries, transform organizations, and drive sustained success.

Decision Making As A Repeatable Skill

Decision-making capability evolves with practice as leaders learn from their successes and missteps. Continuous improvement requires reflecting on past outcomes, identifying what worked and what did not, and how to enhance future decisions. This iterative approach strengthens frameworks for evaluating options and managing risks while maintaining a focus on timely action.

A key aspect of decision making is knowing when to move forward. While diligence and preparation are essential, leaders must avoid delays caused by overanalyzing or excessive deliberation. Once sufficient information has been gathered, leaders must act decisively, demonstrating confidence and ensuring that momentum is preserved. Timely decisions not only prevent inefficiency but also build trust within teams and stakeholders.

Fostering a decision-making culture within the organization enhances its effectiveness. Empowering teams to contribute to decisions promotes collaboration, innovation, and shared accountability. This decentralized approach encourages diverse perspectives and reduces blind spots, ensuring that decisions reflect the collective expertise of the organization. Leaders who instill this culture create an environment where bold, efficient, and well-informed choices propel success at every level.

ESSENTIAL LEADERSHIP SKILL #5: COMMUNICATION

Definition Of Communication

Communication is a leader's ability to effectively convey an idea, plan, or directive to all relevant stakeholders within the organization. This skill encompasses not only the delivery of information but also the ability to listen actively, foster understanding, and engage others in meaningful dialogue.

Effective communication ensures alignment, clarity, and cohesion, driving better collaboration and more impactful outcomes. Leaders who master this skill create environments where transparency thrives, trust is built, and teams feel both informed and empowered to act.

The Vital Importance Of Communication

Effective communication is a staple of strong leadership. It underpins every aspect of a leader's role, from articulating a vision to rallying a team, resolving conflicts, and driving change. A leader who excels in communication fosters trust, inspires action, and ensures that all stakeholders are aligned with the organization's goals and priorities.

1. Building Trust and Credibility

Clear, consistent communication builds trust and credibility. When leaders are transparent and articulate, stakeholders are more likely to have confidence in their decisions and vision. This trust is critical for fostering loyalty and ensuring buy-in, especially during periods of change or uncertainty.

2. Aligning Teams and Objectives

Communication is essential for aligning teams around a shared purpose. Leaders must ensure that employees understand not only what needs to be done but why it matters. This alignment drives accountability, minimizes misunderstandings, and ensures that efforts are directed toward achieving organizational goals.

3. Navigating Complexities

Today's organizations operate in increasingly complex environments. Effective communication helps leaders break down complexity, making strategies and objectives accessible to a diverse range of stakeholders. Leaders who excel in communication can translate intricate ideas into clear, actionable messages that resonate across all levels of the organization.

4. Fostering Collaboration and Engagement

Good communication promotes collaboration by encouraging open dialogue, sharing of ideas, and active listening. Leaders who create an environment where communication flows freely empower their teams to innovate, resolve conflicts, and work together more effectively. Engaged employees are more likely to contribute their best efforts, and effective communication plays a pivotal role in sustaining this engagement.

When leaders communicate with clarity and authenticity, they create a culture where information is shared openly, collaboration flourishes, and employees feel valued.

Key Components Of Communication

To master communication, leaders must integrate several critical components:

- *Clarity:* Communicate in a concise, straightforward way to minimize ambiguity and ensure understanding.

- *Active Listening:* Engage with stakeholders and value feedback to build trust and gather insights.

- *Empathy:* Address the perspectives and emotions of your audience to create meaningful connections.

- *Consistency:* Deliver aligned messages across all channels to reinforce priorities and avoid confusion.

- *Adaptability:* Adjust communication styles to suit different audiences, platforms, and contexts for maximum impact.

By integrating these key components, leaders ensure their messages are effective, meaningful, and strategically aligned with their organizational goals.

Familiar Examples Of Effective Communication

Sara Blakely's Storytelling at Spanx

Sara Blakely, founder of Spanx, is celebrated for her exceptional communication skills, particularly her use of storytelling to connect with employees and customers. By sharing her personal journey of starting the company with $5,000 and a vision, Blakely has built trust, inspired her team, and cultivated a loyal customer base, demonstrating how authentic communication can drive a brand's success.

Indra Nooyi's Transparent Leadership at PepsiCo

As CEO of PepsiCo, Indra Nooyi prioritized open and transparent communication, regularly sharing the company's vision and strategy with employees. Her "Performance with Purpose" framework was clearly articulated, ensuring that employees understood how their work aligned with corporate goals.

Tim Cook's Communication of Apple's Values

As Apple's CEO, Tim Cook is renowned for his ability to communicate the company's core values, particularly its commitment to privacy, innovation, and sustainability. Through clear, consistent messaging, Cook has reinforced Apple's brand identity while earning trust from employees, customers, and stakeholders worldwide.

Each of these leaders demonstrates how communication fosters engagement, trust, and alignment, helping organizations thrive.

Communication As A Repeatable Skill

Communication is a dynamic skill that must evolve alongside shifting organizational needs, technologies, and team structures. Leaders who adapt their communication styles ensure clarity, alignment, and engagement, especially in an increasingly digital and remote work environment.

Mastering multiple communication platforms helps maintain cohesion and foster collaboration across diverse audiences.

Active listening remains central to effective communication. Leaders who encourage open dialogue, solicit feedback, and respond thoughtfully build trust and strengthen teamwork. When communication is interactive rather than one-directional, it fosters transparency, accountability, and shared purpose within the organization.

Cultural and emotional intelligence further enhance communication effectiveness. As workplaces become more diverse, leaders must navigate different communication styles with sensitivity and inclusivity. By prioritizing respect, adaptability, and meaningful connection, leaders create environments where collaboration thrives and teams remain engaged.

ESSENTIAL LEADERSHIP SKILL #6: MOTIVATION

Definition Of Motivation

Motivation is a leader's ability to inspire and energize stakeholders, aligning their efforts with the organization's objectives and fostering sustained engagement. This skill involves cultivating a sense of purpose, creating an environment where people feel valued, and instilling the energy and commitment necessary to achieve ambitious goals.

Effective motivation goes beyond superficial incentives, tapping into the deeper aspirations and values of individuals and teams. Leaders who master motivation empower their organizations to maintain high performance, resilience, and innovation, even in times of uncertainty and change.

The Vital Importance Of Motivation

Motivation is the engine that powers an organization's success. Leaders who excel at motivating stakeholders ensure that employees, partners, and other contributors are not just compliant but fully invested in the organization's mission. This engagement translates to higher productivity, stronger collaboration, and greater resilience in the face of challenges.

1. Driving High Performance

Motivated stakeholders consistently deliver their best work. Leaders who understand how to inspire commitment and enthusiasm create teams that exceed expectations and tackle challenges with determination. Motivation enhances individual and collective performance, directly contributing to organizational success.

2. Enhancing Retention and Loyalty

In a competitive talent market, motivation plays a critical role in retaining top performers. Leaders who foster a supportive, inspiring environment build loyalty among employees and stakeholders. This loyalty reduces turnover and creates a stable foundation for long-term growth.

3. Building Resilience

Motivated teams are better equipped to handle setbacks and adversity. Leaders who inspire confidence and optimism can galvanize their teams to navigate difficult periods with focus and determination. This resilience is a key factor in maintaining momentum during times of uncertainty.

4. Aligning Stakeholders with the Vision

Motivation bridges the gap between strategy and execution by aligning stakeholders with the organization's vision and objectives. Leaders who inspire belief in the mission ensure that everyone is pulling in the same direction, creating synergy and amplifying impact.

By fostering motivation, leaders cultivate an environment where individuals feel empowered, engaged, and committed to achieving shared success.

Key Components Of Motivation

To master motivation, leaders must integrate several critical components:

- *Inspiration:* Share a vision that connects stakeholders to a greater purpose, energizing them to pursue ambitious goals.

- *Recognition:* Celebrate successes and acknowledge contributions to make individuals and teams feel valued.

- *Empathy:* Understand the unique drivers of individuals and teams to tailor motivational strategies effectively.

- *Empowerment:* Provide the tools, autonomy, and support that enable stakeholders to take ownership of their work.

- *Optimism:* Maintain a positive outlook that inspires confidence and resilience, even during challenges.

By leveraging these components, leaders create a culture of motivation that drives both personal and organizational success.

Familiar Examples Of Effective Motivation

Sheryl Sandberg's Motivation at Facebook

As COO of Facebook, Sheryl Sandberg motivated employees by creating an environment of openness and recognition. Her emphasis on empowerment and encouragement helped align the workforce with the company's mission to connect the world.

Richard Branson's Empowerment at Virgin Group

Richard Branson, founder of Virgin Group, has consistently demonstrated motivational leadership by empowering his employees with trust and autonomy. He believes in supporting teams with the freedom to innovate while fostering a culture of fun and collaboration. This approach has motivated employees across Virgin's diverse ventures to excel and embrace the company's adventurous spirit.

Herb Kelleher's Leadership at Southwest Airlines

Herb Kelleher, the co-founder of Southwest Airlines, built a culture of motivation by prioritizing employee satisfaction. By promoting a fun and inclusive environment and recognizing employee contributions, Kelleher inspired loyalty and productivity, driving the company's long-term success.

These examples highlight how motivation, when effectively cultivated, can inspire employees, enhance engagement, and strengthen an organization's competitive advantage.

Motivation As A Repeatable Skill

Motivation is not a static quality but a skill that leaders must continuously develop and refine. As teams evolve and organizational priorities shift, what inspires individuals today may not be as effective tomorrow. Leaders who regularly assess engagement drivers and adjust their approach foster a workplace culture where motivation remains strong, sustainable, and aligned with long-term success.

Sustaining motivation requires a commitment to recognizing and supporting employees in meaningful ways. Leaders who prioritize trust, empowerment, and appreciation create an environment where individuals feel valued and driven to perform at their best. A balanced approach—blending tangible rewards with intrinsic motivators such as purpose and personal growth—ensures that motivation remains consistent even during challenging periods.

Motivational leadership also extends beyond individuals to shape team culture. Leaders who encourage collaboration, celebrate progress, and connect organizational goals to a greater purpose cultivate a workforce that is engaged and inspired. By reinforcing shared values and aspirations, leaders create a sense of belonging and commitment that fuels sustained performance and innovation.

Chapter Summary

This chapter explored the six essential professional skills that form the foundation of effective leadership: visioning, translation, problem solving, decision making, communication, and motivation. These competencies enable leaders to articulate clear goals, turn strategies into action, and inspire teams to achieve success. While these skills are timeless, the chapter highlighted how their application must evolve to address the complexity and speed of today's business environment. Leaders who excel in professional skills can guide their organizations with confidence, even amidst uncertainty and disruption.

The chapter also emphasized the importance of balance, showing how professional skills complement the relational aspects of leadership. Practical examples illustrated how leaders use these skills to set direction, align stakeholders, and maintain focus under pressure. By mastering these competencies, leaders build a strong foundation for navigating change and fostering long-term success.

Building on this foundation, Chapter 4 transitions to the realm of personal skills, which brings critical aspects like authenticity, empathy, and adaptability to leadership. These relational competencies are critical for inspiring trust, fostering collaboration, and leading with resilience in today's diverse and dynamic workplaces.

CHAPTER 4

PERSONAL SKILLS: THE TRAITS THAT TRANSFORM LEADERS

Personal skills form the foundation of human connection and influence in leadership. While technical expertise and strategic proficiency are essential, it is these relational skills that allow leaders to inspire trust, encourage collaboration, and cultivate resilient teams. Often referred to as "soft skills," they are, in reality, powerful drivers of engagement, adaptability, and long-term success.

In today's evolving business landscape, leaders must demonstrate authenticity, emotional intelligence, and the ability to coach and empower their teams. These skills enable leaders to create inclusive environments, build lasting relationships, and navigate challenges with agility. This chapter explores six essential personal skills—coaching, authenticity, emotional intelligence, curiosity, flexibility, and resilience—providing insight into how they can shape leadership effectiveness.

Mastering personal skills is critical for leaders seeking to establish meaningful connections, drive innovation, and cultivate a culture of trust. By developing these attributes, leaders strengthen their ability to guide their teams through uncertainty, inspire loyalty, and ensure that both individuals and organizations thrive in an ever-changing world.

Leadership At A Human Level

While professional skills provide the structure for effective leadership, personal skills bring depth, relatability, and emotional intelligence to the role. These competencies allow leaders to build relationships, navigate interpersonal challenges, and create work environments where individuals feel valued and empowered. Leaders who develop strong personal skills can foster engagement, promote inclusivity, and strengthen collaboration—key traits in today's diverse and fast-moving workplaces.

More than ever, organizations are recognizing that leadership is not just about decision making and strategy but also about connection and influence. Effective leaders must be able to understand and manage emotions, inspire confidence, and communicate in ways that resonate with their teams. The ability to coach employees, exhibit authenticity, and adapt to shifting circumstances is what differentiates exceptional leaders from those who merely manage.

By cultivating personal skills, leaders create workplaces that encourage innovation, psychological safety, and shared purpose. These skills are not innate; they can be developed through conscious effort and self-awareness. The following sections will explore how mastering these capabilities can strengthen leadership impact and improve organizational outcomes.

Why Personal Skills Matter

Personal skills empower leaders to transform their relationships with employees, peers, and stakeholders, creating the conditions for growth and innovation. These skills are vital for:

1. *Building Trust and Collaboration:* Trust is the foundation of any effective team. Personal skills help leaders establish credibility, create openness, and foster genuine connections that enhance collaboration.

2. *Inspiring Through Empathy and Resilience:* Understanding the perspectives and emotions of others enables leaders to motivate their teams and guide them through challenges with compassion and resolve.

3. *Leading Inclusively:* Personal skills encourage inclusivity and respect for diversity, ensuring that all voices are heard and valued in decision-making processes.

4. *Adapting to Change with Poise:* In uncertain times, leaders who exhibit resilience and adaptability inspire confidence, keeping teams aligned and focused.

An Overview Of Personal Skills

This chapter delves into six essential personal skills every contemporary leader must develop:

1. *Coaching:* Empowering others to grow and develop by providing guidance, feedback, and support.

2. *Authenticity:* Leading with integrity by aligning actions with values, building credibility and respect.

3. *Emotional Intelligence:* Understanding and managing emotions—both your own and those of others—to foster trust and collaboration.

4. *Curiosity:* Staying open to new ideas, exploring diverse perspectives, and fostering continuous learning.

5. *Adaptability*: Adjusting strategies and behaviors in response to evolving circumstances and challenges.

6. *Resilience*: Recovering from setbacks with determination and focus, inspiring teams to persevere.

Each of these skills strengthens a leader's ability to connect with others, build high-performing teams, and navigate the complexities of leadership with confidence.

A Comprehensive Review Of The Personal Skills

Each of these skills builds on the others, forming an interconnected framework for leadership excellence. Leaders who develop these competencies can foster collaboration, inspire trust, and create cultures of continuous learning and adaptability.

In the following sections, we will examine each of these six personal skills in detail, beginning with coaching—a foundational ability that enables leaders to nurture growth and unlock potential within their teams.

ESSENTIAL LEADERSHIP SKILL #7: COACHING

Definition Of Coaching

Coaching is a leader's ability to formally or informally develop the skills, competencies, and confidence of individuals within their sphere of influence. This skill extends beyond performance management to fostering growth, enabling individuals to reach their full potential and preparing them for future opportunities. Effective coaching also contributes to succession planning, ensuring that organizations are equipped with a strong pipeline of capable leaders.

Leaders who excel in coaching create an environment where employees feel supported, challenged, and empowered to continuously improve. By prioritizing development, they enhance individual performance while strengthening the overall effectiveness and flexibility of their teams.

The Vital Importance Of Coaching

Coaching is a foundation of sustainable leadership development. Leaders who excel in coaching create environments where individuals and teams thrive, enabling organizations to meet both current challenges and future demands. Coaching empowers employees, drives engagement, and fosters a culture of continuous learning and improvement.

1. Enhancing Individual Performance

Coaching provides personalized guidance that helps individuals identify and address specific areas for improvement. By tailoring feedback and development strategies, leaders enable employees to enhance their performance and achieve their goals. This targeted approach benefits both the individual and the organization by improving productivity and efficiency.

2. Building a Leadership Pipeline

Succession planning is critical for organizational resilience, and coaching plays a vital role in preparing future leaders. By identifying high-potential individuals and mentoring them, leaders ensure that the organization has a steady supply of capable successors ready to take on greater responsibilities.

3. Strengthening Team Dynamics

Coaching promotes trust and collaboration within teams. When leaders invest time in developing their people, they create stronger bonds and a shared commitment to collective success. This improves communication, morale, and alignment with organizational objectives.

4. Driving a Culture of Learning

Coaching helps cultivate a growth mindset within the organization. Employees who experience meaningful development are more likely to seek out new opportunities for learning and innovation. This culture of continuous improvement ensures that the organization remains agile and competitive in a rapidly changing environment.

By mastering coaching, leaders strengthen both individual capabilities and team effectiveness, positioning their organizations for long-term success.

Key Components Of Coaching

To master coaching, leaders must integrate several critical components:

- *Active Listening:* Understand individual needs, goals, and challenges by fully engaging and asking thoughtful questions to uncover deeper insights.

- *Constructive Feedback:* Offer clear, actionable insights that reinforce strengths and address improvement areas, fostering confidence and growth.

- *Empathy:* Build trust by understanding and valuing individuals' perspectives, creating a supportive environment for development.

- *Goal Setting:* Work collaboratively to set realistic, measurable objectives that align personal aspirations with organizational goals.

- *Follow-up:* Regularly check progress, provide support, and adjust as needed to sustain momentum and ensure success.

By leveraging these elements, leaders create a coaching framework that drives personal and professional development.

Familiar Examples Of Effective Coaching

Tobi Lütke's Mentorship at Shopify

Tobi Lütke, CEO and founder of Shopify, exemplifies effective coaching by fostering a culture of learning and empowerment within the rapidly growing e-commerce platform. Lütke invests in the development of his leadership team, encouraging innovation and autonomy while aligning them with Shopify's mission of empowering entrepreneurs globally. His coaching approach has helped create a high-performing team that continues to drive the company's success.

Mary Barra's Development Focus at General Motors

Mary Barra, CEO of General Motors, credits much of her success to mentors who coached her early in her career. As a leader, she has prioritized mentoring others, fostering a culture of development that prepares employees for leadership roles.

Eric Yuan's Team Coaching at Zoom

Eric Yuan, founder and CEO of Zoom, focuses on coaching his team to embrace innovation and customer centricity. By developing his employees' skills and encouraging their growth, Yuan has created a high-performing organization capable of rapid adaptation in the tech sector.

These examples highlight how coaching strengthens leadership, enhances innovation, and builds resilient teams.

Coaching As A Repeatable Skill

Coaching is a dynamic skill that must continually evolve to meet the changing needs of individuals and organizations. Effective leaders refine their approach by reflecting on past experiences, learning new strategies, and staying attuned to the shifting goals and priorities of their teams. Self-awareness and adaptability are critical for maintaining impactful coaching relationships.

As workplaces grow more diverse and global, leaders must integrate cultural intelligence and inclusivity into their coaching practices. Recognizing and respecting individual perspectives ensures that coaching efforts are equitable and resonate across diverse teams. This inclusivity strengthens organizational cohesion and broadens the scope of development opportunities.

Finally, coaching requires balancing immediate performance needs with long-term growth. By focusing on both current challenges and future potential, leaders cultivate resilient teams prepared to navigate change and seize opportunities. Coaching is not just about addressing present issues—it's about building a strong foundation for sustained organizational success.

ESSENTIAL LEADERSHIP SKILL #8: AUTHENTICITY

Definition Of Authenticity

Authenticity is a leader's ability to align their actions with their values and beliefs while remaining transparent, consistent, and ethical. Authentic leaders build trust through genuine behaviors, ensuring that their decisions and leadership style reflect both their personal integrity and the organization's mission. This skill is essential for fostering credibility, strengthening relationships, and creating a workplace culture based on trust and respect.

Authenticity is not about perfection—it is about self-awareness, honesty, and a willingness to lead with integrity, even in challenging situations. Leaders who embrace authenticity cultivate environments where employees feel valued, respected, and motivated to contribute their best.

The Vital Importance Of Authenticity

Authenticity is a hallmark of effective leadership in an era where transparency, trust, and values-driven decision making are increasingly important. Stakeholders—whether employees, customers, or investors—are more likely to support leaders who exhibit genuine commitment to their beliefs and the organization's mission.

1. Building Trust and Credibility

Trust is the cornerstone of leadership, and authenticity is key to building it. Leaders who align their actions with their words demonstrate consistency and reliability, earning the confidence of those they lead. Trust allows leaders to foster deeper connections, inspire loyalty, and create an environment where people feel safe to contribute their best.

2. Enhancing Organizational Culture

Authenticity plays a vital role in shaping a positive organizational culture. Leaders who model genuine behaviors and uphold the organization's values set a powerful example for their teams. This alignment between personal actions and organizational priorities creates a sense of purpose and cohesion that strengthens morale and engagement.

3. Strengthening Decision Making

When leaders act authentically, their decisions are guided by a clear sense of purpose and ethical principles. This alignment ensures that choices are consistent with the organization's values, championing long-term credibility and mitigating risks associated with opportunistic or short-sighted actions.

4. Increasing Resilience During Change

Authentic leadership is particularly crucial during times of change or uncertainty. By communicating openly and demonstrating vulnerability when appropriate, authentic leaders foster trust and confidence, helping their teams navigate challenges with clarity and conviction.

By prioritizing authenticity, leaders create work environments built on trust, respect, and shared purpose.

Key Components Of Authenticity

To master authenticity, leaders must integrate several critical components:

- *Self-awareness:* Understand your beliefs, values, and motivations, and ensure they align with organizational goals to make authentic decisions.

- *Transparency:* Be open about intentions, decisions, and challenges to build trust and foster a culture of openness.

- *Integrity:* Act consistently with your values, even under pressure, to set an ethical example and inspire trust.

- *Empathy:* Show genuine care by understanding the perspectives and needs of others, strengthening relationships and support.

- *Consistency:* Match actions to words to reinforce trust, build respect, and create a stable foundation for success.

When leaders embody these elements, they create an authentic leadership style that resonates with employees and stakeholders alike.

Familiar Examples Of Effective Authenticity

The Volkswagen Board's Response to the Emissions Scandal

Following the diesel emissions scandal, Volkswagen's board of directors took steps to rebuild trust and demonstrate authenticity by openly acknowledging the company's failures. The board implemented sweeping reforms, committed to greater transparency, and prioritized investments in sustainable technologies, signaling a genuine shift in values and direction.

Ginni Rometty's Leadership at IBM

During her tenure as CEO of IBM, Ginni Rometty demonstrated authenticity by addressing challenges openly and aligning the company's transformation with her personal commitment to innovation and inclusion. Her transparent communication and values-driven decisions helped IBM adapt to a rapidly evolving tech landscape.

Howard Schultz's Return to Starbucks

During Starbucks' financial struggles in 2008, CEO Howard Schultz demonstrated authenticity by reconnecting with the company's core values of quality and community. He openly acknowledged challenges, closed 7,000 stores for barista retraining, and reinforced commitments to ethical sourcing, restoring trust and revitalizing the brand.

These examples highlight how authentic leadership fosters resilience, trust, and long-term success.

Authenticity As A Repeatable Skill

Authenticity is not a fixed trait but a skill that requires continuous reflection and reinforcement. Leaders must regularly assess whether their behaviors align with their stated values and commitments. When leaders demonstrate consistency in their decisions and actions, they reinforce trust and credibility over time.

Being authentic also requires a willingness to embrace vulnerability. Leaders who acknowledge challenges, admit mistakes, and show humility earn greater respect from their teams. However, authenticity must be backed by consistent follow-through—leaders must ensure that their words are supported by meaningful action.

Finally, authenticity in leadership must be adaptable to different environments and cultural contexts. While staying true to one's values, leaders must also recognize and respect diverse perspectives to foster inclusion and collaboration. By acting with integrity while remaining flexible in communication and leadership style, authentic leaders create lasting impact and drive meaningful organizational success.

ESSENTIAL LEADERSHIP SKILL #9: EMOTIONAL INTELLIGENCE

Definition Of Emotional Intelligence

Emotional intelligence is a leader's ability to recognize, manage, and respond effectively to both their own emotions and the emotions of those around them. This skill encompasses self-awareness, self-regulation, empathy, social awareness, and strong relationship management. Leaders with high emotional intelligence create stronger connections, navigate conflicts with composure, and foster environments built on trust and collaboration.

Unlike technical expertise, which focuses on knowledge and execution, emotional intelligence enables leaders to inspire and engage people. By mastering EI, leaders can build high-performing teams, strengthen organizational culture, and navigate complex interpersonal dynamics with confidence.

The Vital Importance Of Emotional Intelligence

In modern leadership, emotional intelligence is increasingly recognized as a critical differentiator between good and great leaders. It enables leaders to maintain composure under pressure, build meaningful relationships, and inspire teams to achieve their potential. While technical and professional skills are important, emotional intelligence is the foundation for leading people effectively.

1. Building Strong Relationships

Leaders who exhibit emotional intelligence develop deeper and more meaningful connections with their teams, peers, and stakeholders. By understanding and respecting others' perspectives, emotionally intelligent leaders foster trust and collaboration, creating a unified and supportive work environment.

2. Managing Conflict Effectively

Conflict is inevitable in any organization, but leaders with high emotional intelligence handle disagreements constructively. They remain calm, listen actively, and seek solutions that satisfy all parties involved, minimizing disruption and preserving relationships.

3. Enhancing Decision Making

Emotional intelligence enhances decision making by enabling leaders to recognize and regulate their emotions. By approaching decisions with a clear and balanced mindset, leaders can evaluate options objectively, avoiding impulsive or emotionally driven choices that may harm the organization.

4. Inspiring and Motivating Teams

Leaders with emotional intelligence inspire their teams by demonstrating empathy and understanding. When employees feel heard and valued, they are more engaged and motivated to perform at their best. This creates a culture of trust and mutual respect, which drives organizational success.

By integrating emotional intelligence into their leadership approach, leaders can strengthen relationships, resolve conflicts, and create a more engaged and productive workforce.

Key Components Of Emotional Intelligence

To master emotional intelligence, leaders must develop several critical components:

- *Self-awareness:* Recognize your emotions, triggers, and behaviors, and understand how they influence your decisions and interactions.

- *Self-regulation:* Manage emotional responses to stay composed and choose measured reactions that align with your goals.

- *Empathy:* Understand and respond to others' emotions, building trust and creating an inclusive, supportive environment.

- *Social Skills:* Build strong relationships, resolve conflicts, and motivate teams through clear communication and collaboration.

- *Adaptability:* Adjust emotional responses and behaviors to remain effective in changing situations and with diverse individuals.

When leaders cultivate these skills, they enhance their ability to lead with confidence, influence others positively, and drive meaningful change within their organizations.

Familiar Examples Of Effective Emotional Intelligence

Brian Chesky's Leadership at Airbnb

Brian Chesky, co-founder and CEO of Airbnb, demonstrated exceptional emotional intelligence during the COVID-19 pandemic. Faced with significant disruptions to the travel industry, Chesky led with transparency and empathy by openly communicating with employees and stakeholders. His thoughtful handling of layoffs, which included generous severance packages and support for finding new jobs, showcased his ability to balance business decisions with compassion.

Reshma Saujani's Leadership at Girls Who Code

Reshma Saujani, founder of Girls Who Code, exemplifies emotional intelligence through her advocacy for women in technology. Saujani's empathetic leadership focuses on understanding the unique challenges faced by underrepresented groups and creating programs that empower young women to succeed. Her genuine connection with her mission and team has fueled the organization's growth and impact.

Tony Hsieh's Leadership at Zappos

The late Tony Hsieh, former CEO of Zappos, built a company culture centered on emotional intelligence. His focus on employee happiness and meaningful connections created a workplace that thrived on collaboration, engagement, and exceptional customer service.

These examples highlight how emotionally intelligent leadership enhances decision making, strengthens relationships, and fosters cultures of trust and collaboration.

Emotional Intelligence As A Repeatable Skill

Emotional intelligence is not an innate trait—it is a skill that leaders can develop and refine over time. By regularly reflecting on emotional responses and their impact, leaders can enhance their ability to connect with and support their teams. Through active self-awareness and self-regulation, leaders can maintain composure, make thoughtful decisions, and model emotional intelligence for others.

Developing emotional intelligence also requires vulnerability and authenticity. Leaders who are willing to admit mistakes, share challenges, and demonstrate genuine care for their teams build credibility and trust. This openness fosters stronger relationships and enhances a leader's ability to inspire and influence effectively.

In today's diverse and dynamic workplace, emotional intelligence is essential for leading across cultures and generations. Leaders must navigate different communication styles, workplace expectations, and perspectives with empathy and adaptability. By prioritizing emotional intelligence, leaders can create environments where people feel valued, motivated, and empowered to contribute to long-term organizational success.

ESSENTIAL LEADERSHIP SKILL #10: CURIOSITY

Definition Of Curiosity

Curiosity is a leader's ability to remain actively engaged in learning about their surroundings, challenges, and opportunities. It reflects a willingness to ask insightful questions, explore diverse perspectives, and seek deeper understanding. Leaders who cultivate curiosity foster a mindset of continuous learning and discovery, allowing them to adapt, innovate, and make well-informed decisions.

More than just an intellectual pursuit, curiosity is a leadership advantage that drives exploration, challenges assumptions, and encourages breakthrough thinking. By remaining open to new ideas and actively questioning the status quo, curious leaders inspire a culture of growth and innovation within their organizations.

The Vital Importance Of Curiosity

Curiosity is a foundational leadership trait in a world of rapid change and increasing complexity. Leaders who are curious continuously expand their knowledge, uncover opportunities, and remain agile in the face of uncertainty. Curiosity drives exploration and experimentation, allowing organizations to stay ahead of industry trends and maintain a competitive edge.

1. Driving Innovation

Curious leaders encourage creative thinking and exploration within their organizations. By questioning the status quo and remaining open to new ideas, they foster an environment where innovation thrives. This willingness to explore uncharted territories often leads to breakthrough solutions and strategies that differentiate the organization in the marketplace.

2. Enhancing Decision Making

Curiosity prompts leaders to gather more information, consult diverse viewpoints, and analyze situations from multiple angles. This deeper understanding enables more informed decision making, reducing the risks associated with assumptions or incomplete data. Curious leaders are better equipped to navigate uncertainty and complexity with confidence.

3. Building Collaborative Relationships

Leaders who ask thoughtful, genuine questions demonstrate interest in others' perspectives and expertise. This builds trust, bolsters collaboration, and creates an inclusive environment where team members feel valued. Curiosity strengthens relationships and encourages open dialogue, leading to better teamwork and collective problem solving.

4. Cultivating Continuous Learning

Curiosity drives lifelong learning, a critical trait for leaders who wish to stay relevant in dynamic industries. By remaining open to new knowledge, technologies, and approaches, curious leaders ensure that they and their organizations remain adaptable and competitive in a rapidly evolving landscape.

By integrating curiosity into their leadership style, leaders encourage adaptability, strengthen relationships, and foster a culture of learning that supports long-term success.

Key Components Of Curiosity

To master curiosity, leaders must integrate several critical components:

- *Genuine Questioning:* Ask open-ended, thought-provoking questions to explore new ideas, uncover insights, and encourage others to share their perspectives.

- *Active Listening:* Pay close attention to responses, clarify understanding, and use the insights gained to build rapport and create deeper connections.

- *Exploration:* Actively seek knowledge from diverse sources, including research, feedback, collaboration, and unconventional perspectives, to expand understanding.

- *Adaptability:* Embrace uncertainty and the discomfort of discovery, remaining open to unexpected insights and changing directions when necessary.

- *Humility:* Recognize that no matter your expertise or position, there is always more to learn, and value the contributions of others to your growth.

By integrating these components, leaders create an environment where curiosity is not only encouraged but also embedded into the organization's DNA.

Familiar Examples Of Effective Curiosity

Ellen Kullman's Strategic Curiosity at DuPont

As CEO of DuPont, Ellen Kullman demonstrated exceptional curiosity by exploring how the company's legacy of innovation could meet modern challenges. Her focus on understanding emerging industries, such as renewable energy and advanced materials, enabled DuPont to pivot toward sustainable solutions, ensuring its relevance in a rapidly evolving market.

Tristan Walker's Vision at Walker & Company Brands

Tristan Walker, founder and CEO of Walker & Company Brands, showcased curiosity by delving deeply into the unmet needs of underrepresented communities in the personal care market. By asking insightful questions about the unique grooming challenges faced by people of color, he developed Bevel, a shaving system specifically designed for coarse or curly hair. Walker's curiosity about his customers' experiences not only addressed a neglected market but also created a loyal customer base that values authenticity and inclusion.

Melanie Perkins's Curiosity at Canva

Melanie Perkins, co-founder and CEO of Canva, displayed remarkable curiosity by identifying gaps in the design software market. Her persistent questioning about how to make graphic design tools more accessible to non-designers led to the creation of Canva's user-friendly platform, which has revolutionized visual content creation and empowered millions worldwide.

These examples demonstrate how curiosity leads to business transformation, customer-centric innovation, and long-term growth.

Curiosity As A Repeatable Skill

Curiosity is not an innate trait but a skill that leaders can develop through intentional practice. By approaching challenges with an open mind, leaders can set aside biases and preconceptions, allowing for the discovery of fresh insights and creative solutions. This mindset unlocks new opportunities for growth and continuous improvement.

Fostering curiosity also requires creating a workplace culture that values exploration and learning. Leaders can model curiosity by encouraging experimentation, asking thought-provoking questions, and recognizing employees who challenge assumptions. This approach strengthens collective problem solving and drives innovation at all levels of the organization.

In an increasingly interconnected world, curiosity demands cultural awareness and a willingness to embrace diverse perspectives. Leaders who seek to understand others' viewpoints and adjust to different contexts expand their horizons and strengthen relationships. This ability positions both leaders and organizations to thrive in dynamic and complex environments.

ESSENTIAL LEADERSHIP SKILL #11: ADAPTABILITY

Definition Of Adaptability

Adaptability is a leader's ability to adjust to evolving circumstances, both within their organization and in the external market. This skill involves recognizing shifts, responding with agility, and maintaining effectiveness despite uncertainty or disruption. Adaptable leaders pivot strategies, embrace innovation, and guide their organizations through both challenges and opportunities.

More than simply reacting to change, adaptability is a proactive approach to leadership. Leaders who cultivate this skill continuously assess trends, anticipate disruptions, and refine their strategies to ensure sustained success.

The Vital Importance Of Adaptability

Adaptability has become a defining skill for contemporary leaders, especially in an era marked by rapid technological advancements, evolving workforce dynamics, and volatile market conditions. Leaders who can adapt effectively not only position their organizations for success but also model resilience and flexibility for their teams.

1. Navigating Change

Change is inevitable, whether it stems from market disruptions, regulatory shifts, or internal organizational evolution. Leaders who embrace adaptability view change as an opportunity rather than a threat. This perspective allows them to respond proactively, maintain momentum, and steer their organizations toward growth despite uncertainty.

2. Encouraging Innovation

Adaptability encourages a mindset of experimentation and openness to new ideas. Leaders who are willing to evolve their strategies and explore unconventional approaches create an environment where innovation flourishes. This capacity to innovate is critical for staying competitive in dynamic industries.

3. Supporting Team Resilience

Adaptable leaders inspire confidence and stability in their teams even during times of upheaval. By modeling flexibility and a solutions-focused mindset, they help employees remain engaged, motivated, and productive. This resilience contributes to stronger team cohesion and a more agile organizational culture.

4. Aligning with Evolving Stakeholder Expectations

As stakeholder priorities shift—whether they relate to sustainability, diversity, or technological integration—leaders must adjust their strategies to align with these expectations. Adaptability ensures that leaders remain attuned to stakeholder needs, strengthening trust and relationships over time.

By integrating adaptability into their leadership approach, leaders create organizations that can thrive in an ever-changing business landscape.

Key Components Of Adaptability

To master adaptability, leaders must develop several critical components:

- *Situational Awareness:* Continuously monitor and interpret changes in both the external and internal environments to stay informed and proactive in addressing emerging trends and challenges.

- *Agility:* Respond quickly and effectively to new challenges and opportunities by adjusting strategies, processes, and decisions as needed to maintain momentum and achieve objectives.

- *Resilience:* Maintain focus, composure, and determination in the face of uncertainty, setbacks, or adversity, ensuring that both you and your team stay motivated and aligned.

- *Continuous Learning:* Stay open to new information, perspectives, and approaches, using each as an opportunity to refine your skills and acclimatize to evolving conditions.

- *Forward-thinking:* Anticipate potential changes and challenges, proactively preparing strategies and resources to ensure you are ready to respond effectively.

By integrating these components, leaders ensure their ability to pivot effectively while maintaining clarity and strategic direction.

Familiar Examples Of Effective Adaptability

Patagonia's Commitment to Sustainability

Patagonia's leadership has consistently adapted to align with environmental priorities and shifting consumer expectations. By embedding sustainability into its core business model, the company has remained innovative and relevant, fostering a strong and loyal customer base.

Peloton's Product Evolution

Peloton demonstrated adaptability by expanding beyond stationary bikes to offer a wider range of fitness products and digital content. In response to changing consumer needs, the company diversified its offerings, including treadmills and strength training equipment, while enhancing its subscription platform to remain competitive.

Warby Parker's Shift to Omnichannel Retail

Warby Parker initially gained traction as a direct-to-consumer brand, but its leadership showed adaptability by integrating brick-and-mortar stores to complement its online presence. This hybrid model allowed the company to better serve customers and remain resilient amid market shifts.

These examples highlight how adaptability enables organizations to navigate disruptions while seizing new opportunities.

Adaptability As A Repeatable Skill

Adaptability is not a one-time adjustment but an ongoing process that leaders must actively refine. Regularly assessing trends, evaluating strategies, and embracing feedback ensures leaders remain effective in ever-changing environments. This vigilance allows them to respond proactively to both challenges and opportunities.

Cultivating adaptability also requires stepping outside comfort zones. Leaders must be open to experimenting with new approaches, learning from failures, and adjusting tactics as needed. This combination of humility and resilience is essential for navigating the complexities of modern leadership while maintaining forward momentum.

Finally, adaptable leaders foster cultures of flexibility within their organizations. By empowering teams to experiment and pivot as necessary, they create environments where change is embraced rather than resisted. This cultural alignment enhances both individual and collective agility, positioning organizations for long-term success in dynamic landscapes.

ESSENTIAL LEADERSHIP SKILL #12: RESILIENCE

Definition Of Resilience

Resilience is a leader's ability to recover quickly from setbacks and hardships while maintaining focus and composure in the face of adversity. This skill ensures that leaders can navigate challenges effectively, safeguard their organization's stability, and continue driving progress toward long-term objectives.

Resilience is not just about enduring difficulties—it's about learning from them, adapting, and emerging stronger. It requires mental toughness, emotional balance, and a solutions-focused mindset that transforms obstacles into opportunities for growth.

The Vital Importance Of Resilience

Resilience is one of the most critical leadership skills in today's unpredictable and high-pressure business environment. Whether dealing with economic disruptions, operational failures, or personal challenges, resilient leaders provide the steadiness and direction necessary to keep their organizations on course.

1. Maintaining Organizational Stability

In moments of crisis or uncertainty, resilient leaders act as anchors, providing reassurance to employees, stakeholders, and customers. Their ability to remain calm and focused prevents panic and boosts confidence, ensuring that the organization can weather storms without losing momentum.

2. Sustaining Long-term Progress

Setbacks are inevitable in any endeavor, but resilient leaders use these moments as opportunities to recalibrate and refocus. Rather than dwelling on failures, they emphasize learning and improvement, enabling their teams to recover and continue advancing toward strategic goals.

3. Inspiring Teams Through Adversity

Leaders with resilience serve as role models for their teams, demonstrating that challenges can be overcome with determination and perseverance. This mindset encourages employees to adopt a similar attitude, fostering a culture of optimism, grit, and accountability.

4. Building Adaptive Organizations

Resilience at the leadership level promotes organizational adaptability. Resilient leaders are better equipped to make strategic pivots, innovate under pressure, and seize opportunities that emerge from adversity.

This adaptability ensures that the organization remains competitive in a rapidly evolving landscape.

By strengthening their resilience, leaders cultivate stability, innovation, and perseverance throughout their organizations.

Key Components Of Resilience

To master resilience, leaders must cultivate several critical components:

- *Emotional Regulation*: Effectively manage stress and maintain composure during challenging situations, ensuring that emotional responses do not cloud judgment or decision making.

- *Optimism*: Cultivate a mindset focused on solutions and opportunities, inspiring confidence by framing challenges as possibilities for growth rather than insurmountable obstacles.

- *Self-awareness*: Recognize personal limits and understand when to seek support or delegate tasks, ensuring sustainable performance while maintaining a balanced perspective.

- *Adaptability*: Adjust strategies and behaviors to navigate changing circumstances while staying aligned with long-term goals and organizational priorities.

- *Perseverance*: Demonstrate unwavering commitment to achieving objectives, using setbacks as learning experiences to refine approaches and strengthen resolve.

By integrating these components, leaders build resilience as a skill that strengthens both personal and organizational effectiveness.

Familiar Examples Of Effective Resilience

Dara Khosrowshahi's Leadership at Uber

As CEO of Uber, Dara Khosrowshahi has displayed exceptional resilience by guiding the company through significant challenges, including regulatory hurdles, public relations crises, and the global disruption caused by the COVID-19 pandemic. His focus on rebuilding trust, implementing reforms, and driving innovation has helped stabilize Uber and position it for sustained growth.

Feike Sijbesma's Role at Royal DSM

As former CEO and current board member of Royal DSM, Feike Sijbesma exemplified resilience by leading the company's transformation from a bulk chemicals producer to a global leader in nutrition and sustainable solutions. His forward-thinking and ability to navigate challenges helped DSM thrive in rapidly changing markets.

Whitney Wolfe Herd's Founding of Bumble

Whitney Wolfe Herd demonstrated resilience after leaving Tinder amid legal disputes and personal challenges. She channeled her experiences into founding Bumble, a dating app where women initiate conversations, turning adversity into an opportunity to innovate in the tech and relationship industries.

These examples highlight how resilience allows leaders to transform setbacks into catalysts for growth and innovation.

Resilience As A Repeatable Skill

Resilience is not an inherent trait—it is a skill that leaders can develop through experience, reflection, and intentional practice. By analyzing past challenges and identifying effective coping strategies, leaders build the mental and emotional habits necessary to recover quickly from setbacks and maintain focus.

Sustaining resilience requires a commitment to self-care and stress management. Leaders who prioritize their well-being can maintain the energy and composure needed to guide their teams effectively, even in prolonged challenges. Balancing personal and professional demands ensures resilience remains a consistent leadership strength.

Resilient leaders also cultivate resilience within their teams and organizations by fostering a culture that views challenges as opportunities for growth. Encouraging collaboration, creativity, and perseverance builds a workplace where adversity strengthens, rather than weakens, collective performance. This mindset ensures long-term success, stability, and the ability to thrive in uncertain environments.

Chapter Summary

This chapter examined the six essential personal skills that transform leaders into relational and adaptive connectors: coaching, authenticity, emotional intelligence, curiosity, adaptability, and resilience. These skills help leaders inspire trust, foster collaboration, and create inclusive environments where teams feel supported and motivated. The chapter emphasized the growing importance of empathy and adaptability in today's dynamic workplaces, where building meaningful connections is crucial to leading effectively.

Through practical examples, the chapter demonstrated how leaders can develop these skills to manage interpersonal dynamics, navigate uncertainty, and create a culture of trust and innovation. By integrating these traits into their leadership approach, leaders are better equipped to connect with diverse teams and inspire confidence in even the most challenging circumstances.

The next chapter transitions to the critical domain of technology skills, which empower leaders to harness innovation and leverage digital tools to drive organizational success. These skills are indispensable for navigating the rapid technological advancements shaping today's business environment.

CHAPTER 5

TECHNOLOGY SKILLS: LEADING IN A DIGITAL AND DATA-DRIVEN WORLD

As the pace of technological advancement accelerates, leadership is no longer defined solely by strategic vision and interpersonal connection. Leaders must now navigate a digital landscape where innovation and data drive competitive advantage. Technology skills have become indispensable for modern leaders, enabling them to harness emerging tools, make data-informed decisions, and guide their organizations through digital transformation.

This chapter explores three essential technology skills: technology awareness, technology objectivity, and technology application. These competencies equip leaders to stay informed about technological trends, evaluate solutions critically, and implement innovations that align with strategic goals. In a world where the ability to leverage technology often determines organizational success, these skills are no longer optional—they are fundamental.

Through actionable insights and real-world examples, this chapter highlights how leaders can embrace technology as a catalyst for innovation, efficiency, and growth. By mastering these skills, leaders position themselves to stay ahead of disruption and create value in a data-driven world.

Leadership In The Age Of Innovation

Technology has revolutionized how businesses operate, communicate, and compete. For contemporary leaders, mastering technology skills is no longer an advantage—it is a necessity. These competencies bridge the gap between technological advancements and strategic execution, ensuring that organizations remain competitive in a rapidly evolving digital landscape.

Modern leadership requires more than a basic understanding of digital tools. Leaders must be able to identify emerging trends, evaluate potential risks and opportunities, and make informed decisions about technological investments. The ability to integrate technology into workflows, promote digital transformation, and lead teams through change is now a critical aspect of leadership success.

By cultivating technology skills, leaders gain the ability to make data-driven decisions, optimize efficiency, and create cultures of innovation. This chapter explores how these skills empower leaders to unlock new opportunities and sustain competitive advantages in a world where technology continuously reshapes industries.

Why Technology Skills Are Critical

Technology skills give leaders the ability to leverage innovation effectively, ensuring their organizations thrive in the face of disruption. These skills are crucial for:

1. *Driving Digital Transformation:* Leaders must understand how to integrate new technologies into workflows to enhance efficiency and outcomes.

2. *Making Data-driven Decisions:* Technology skills enable leaders to analyze and act on data insights, creating strategies informed by evidence.

3. *Fostering Innovation:* By embracing emerging technologies, leaders can create environments where experimentation and creativity flourish.

4. *Building Organizational Agility:* Technology skills help leaders pivot quickly in response to market changes, positioning their organizations for long-term success.

An Overview Of Technology Skills

This chapter explores three essential technology skills that every leader must master:

1. *Technology Awareness:* Staying informed about emerging tools and understanding their potential applications.

2. *Technology Objectivity:* Evaluating technologies critically and choosing solutions that align with organizational needs.

3. *Technology Application:* Turning technological possibilities into actionable strategies that drive value and impact.

Each of these skills plays a distinct yet interconnected role in shaping a leader's ability to successfully integrate technology into their organization. By mastering these competencies, leaders can create an agile and innovation-driven culture that thrives amid rapid digital transformation.

A Comprehensive Review Of The Technology Skills

Each of these technology skills contributes to a leader's ability to navigate complexity, propel innovation, and make informed strategic decisions. While technology itself is constantly evolving, the ability to critically assess and apply it remains a timeless leadership competency.

In the following sections, we will examine each of these three technology skills in detail, beginning with technology awareness—the foundational ability to stay informed about emerging tools and their potential impact.

ESSENTIAL LEADERSHIP SKILL #13: TECHNOLOGY AWARENESS

Definition Of Technology Awareness

Technology awareness is a leader's ability to absorb the appropriate amount of detail about contemporary technologies that can substantively impact their organization. This skill enables leaders to identify emerging tools, understand their potential applications, and align technological advancements with strategic objectives.

In today's digital landscape, leaders do not need to be technologists, but they must develop a foundational understanding of how key innovations—such as artificial intelligence and cloud computing—can shape their industry. Effective technology awareness ensures that leaders can make informed decisions about adopting, integrating, and leveraging technology to drive innovation and maintain competitive advantage.

The Vital Importance Of Technology Awareness

In an era dominated by rapid technological advancements, technology awareness is no longer optional for leaders—it is indispensable. The ability to understand and evaluate technologies such as AI, cloud computing, blockchain, and IoT equips leaders to navigate opportunities and risks effectively. Leaders who cultivate technology awareness position their organizations to innovate, adapt, and thrive in an increasingly digital marketplace.

1. Driving Innovation and Growth

Technology awareness enables leaders to recognize transformative tools and trends that can revolutionize their industries. By staying informed, leaders can proactively explore new ways to enhance efficiency, deliver value to customers, and unlock growth opportunities.

2. Mitigating Risks and Disruption

Leaders who understand the implications of contemporary technologies are better equipped to anticipate potential challenges, including cyber-security threats, regulatory compliance issues, and ethical concerns. Technology awareness allows leaders to implement safeguards and strategies that protect their organizations from unnecessary risks.

3. Enhancing Decision Making

Leaders with technology awareness can effectively bridge the gap between technical experts and organizational strategy. By absorbing sufficient details about emerging technologies, leaders can assess their relevance, feasibility, and alignment with business objectives, ensuring that decisions about technology investments are informed and impactful.

4. Fostering a Culture of Innovation

Technology awareness empowers leaders to create a culture that embraces digital transformation and innovation. By championing the exploration and adoption of new tools, leaders inspire their teams to think creatively and remain open to change, building organizational resilience in the face of disruption.

By strengthening their technology awareness, leaders enable their organizations to stay ahead of digital trends and remain competitive.

Key Components Of Technology Awareness

To master technology awareness, leaders must integrate several critical components:

- *Curiosity:* Actively maintain an interest in emerging technologies, exploring their potential applications and staying informed about industry advancements to identify opportunities for innovation.

- *Relevance Assessment:* Focus on evaluating technologies that align with organizational goals, industry trends, and specific business needs to ensure that resources are directed toward impactful solutions.

- *Collaboration:* Engage with technical experts and cross-functional teams to deepen understanding, refine strategies, and bridge the gap between technological possibilities and organizational objectives.

- *Adaptability:* Remain open to integrating new tools and adjusting processes as technology evolves, ensuring that the organization stays competitive and responsive to change.

- *Ethical Consideration:* Balance innovation with responsibility, evaluating the societal and ethical implications of technology adoption to align actions with organizational values and stakeholder expectations.

By integrating these components, leaders develop a strategic mindset toward technology, ensuring that innovation aligns with business priorities.

Familiar Examples Of Effective Technology Awareness

Sundar Pichai's Leadership at Google

As CEO of Alphabet Inc. and Google, Sundar Pichai has demonstrated exceptional technology awareness by prioritizing advancements in artificial intelligence and machine learning. Under his leadership, Google has integrated AI across its platforms, including search, advertising, and smart home technologies, while also ensuring that the ethical implications of AI development remain a central focus.

Shantanu Narayen's Leadership at Adobe

As CEO, Shantanu Narayen demonstrated remarkable technology awareness by steering Adobe toward a cloud-based subscription model with Adobe Creative Cloud. This shift embraced the potential of cloud computing and digital transformation, positioning Adobe as a leader in creative and marketing software.

Ajay Banga's Digital Focus at Mastercard

During his tenure as CEO of Mastercard, Ajay Banga demonstrated outstanding technology awareness by driving the company's transition to a digital-first strategy. By investing in AI, cybersecurity, and contactless payment technologies, Banga transformed Mastercard into a leader in digital payments, ensuring its relevance in an increasingly cashless global economy.

These examples illustrate how technology-aware leaders position their organizations for long-term success by embracing innovation strategically.

Technology Awareness As A Repeatable Skill

Technology awareness requires a mindset of continuous learning and exploration. Leaders need to stay informed about emerging trends and assess their relevance to organizational goals. This involves engaging with industry insights, collaborating with technical experts, and remaining curious about new possibilities. By doing so, leaders can proactively position their organizations to leverage innovation effectively.

Prioritization is essential in technology awareness. With the rapid pace of innovation, leaders must discern which technologies align most closely with their strategies and avoid being distracted by tools that do not add value. This focus ensures resources are allocated efficiently and that adoption efforts drive tangible business outcomes.

Ethical and cultural considerations are also integral to technology awareness. Leaders must evaluate the societal impact of technology adoption, balancing innovation with responsibility. This approach ensures organizations remain trusted, inclusive, and aligned with stakeholder expectations, fostering sustainable success in an ever-evolving digital landscape.

ESSENTIAL LEADERSHIP SKILL #14: TECHNOLOGY OBJECTIVITY

Definition Of Technology Objectivity

Technology objectivity is a leader's ability to remain neutral and unbiased when evaluating and selecting rapidly evolving technologies that can best serve the organization's objectives. This skill involves prioritizing the needs and goals of the organization over personal preferences, industry hype, or external pressures. Leaders with technology objectivity make strategic, informed decisions that maximize value and minimize risks associated with adopting or ignoring emerging tools.

In a world where technological advancements are constant, leaders must approach innovation with a critical eye, ensuring that new tools align with business needs rather than being driven by trends. Effective technology objectivity enables organizations to invest wisely, optimize efficiency, and maintain a competitive edge without falling victim to unnecessary complexity or short-lived fads.

The Vital Importance Of Technology Objectivity

In a world of rapid technological advancement, leaders are constantly faced with decisions about which technologies to adopt, invest in, or avoid. Technology objectivity ensures that these decisions are guided by strategic considerations rather than hype, emotional attachment, or vendor influence. Leaders who cultivate this skill help their organizations maintain focus, allocate resources wisely, and avoid the pitfalls of chasing fleeting trends.

1. Aligning Technology with Strategic Objectives

Objectivity allows leaders to evaluate technologies based on their potential to advance organizational goals. This alignment ensures that resources are directed toward tools and platforms that enhance efficiency, drive innovation, or create competitive advantages, rather than those adopted for the sake of novelty.

2. Avoiding the Pitfalls of Hype

The technology landscape is often dominated by buzzwords and trends that can distract from strategic priorities. Leaders with objectivity critically assess the relevance and feasibility of emerging technologies, avoiding costly investments in tools that fail to deliver meaningful impact.

3. Ensuring Fair Evaluation

Technology objectivity promotes fairness in the evaluation process. Leaders who remain neutral create a level playing field for vendors, internal proposals, and competing solutions. This fosters transparency and ensures that the best-fit technology is chosen based on merit rather than external pressures or internal biases.

4. Managing Organizational Risks

Adopting technology without careful evaluation can expose organizations to financial, operational, and reputational risks. Objectivity enables leaders to assess potential downsides, weigh alternatives, and select technologies that align with long-term sustainability and ethical standards.

By maintaining technology objectivity, leaders make strategic choices that strengthen the organization's foundation and long-term success.

Key Components Of Technology Objectivity

To master technology objectivity, leaders must integrate several critical components:

- *Neutrality:* Set aside personal preferences, vendor bias, and external pressures to evaluate technologies impartially, ensuring decisions are based on their merit and organizational relevance.

- *Strategic Focus:* Prioritize technologies that align directly with the organization's goals, objectives, and long-term vision while delivering measurable and impactful outcomes.

- *Data-driven Analysis:* Use evidence, performance metrics, and cost-benefit evaluations to objectively assess the feasibility and potential value of various technological options.

- *Ethical Consideration:* Evaluate the broader societal, stakeholder, and environmental implications of adopting a technology, balancing innovation with responsibility and sustainability.

- *Flexibility:* Stay open to evolving tools, trends, and data, and be willing to revisit and adjust decisions as new information and opportunities arise.

By integrating these components, leaders ensure that their approach to technology remains grounded in logic, fairness, and strategic intent.

Familiar Examples Of Effective Technology Objectivity

Walmart's Technology Transformation

Walmart has demonstrated technology objectivity by carefully selecting tools that primarily enhance its supply chain efficiency and customer experience. From robotics in distribution centers to AI-driven inventory management, Walmart's choices are guided by strategic goals rather than adopting every new trend.

NASA's Balanced Approach to Innovation

NASA consistently exemplifies technology objectivity by evaluating cutting-edge technologies for their ability to meet mission-critical needs. By conducting rigorous testing and analysis, NASA ensures that its investments in innovations—like autonomous rovers or reusable spacecraft—align with long-term exploration goals.

Procter & Gamble's Data-driven Tech Adoption

P&G has shown technology objectivity by integrating only those digital tools that, regardless of vendor, drive measurable outcomes in product development, supply chain management, and consumer engagement. This disciplined approach has enabled the company to maintain agility while avoiding wasteful investments.

These examples illustrate how objectivity in technology decision making prevents unnecessary risk and promotes long-term success.

Technology Objectivity As A Repeatable Skill

Technology objectivity requires leaders to consistently maintain vigilance and balance when evaluating emerging tools. Staying informed about technological advancements while aligning decisions with organizational goals ensures that resources are allocated effectively. By resisting biases and trends, leaders can make choices that are forward-thinking yet grounded in strategic priorities.

Collaboration is key to cultivating objectivity. Engaging cross-functional teams, including technical experts and stakeholders, provides diverse perspectives that reduce blind spots and enhance the decision-making process. This inclusive approach ensures that technology selections are robust and meet both technical and organizational needs.

Leaders must also consider ethical and sustainability implications as part of their evaluations. By weighing the long-term impact of technology choices on society and the environment, leaders align innovation with organizational values and stakeholder trust. This holistic approach fosters responsible decision making and positions organizations for sustainable success in a dynamic landscape.

ESSENTIAL LEADERSHIP SKILL #15: TECHNOLOGY APPLICATION

Definition Of Technology Application

Technology application is a leader's ability to translate technological capabilities into practical uses tailored to the organization's unique needs. This skill bridges the gap between potential and execution by ensuring that technology investments deliver measurable value. Leaders proficient in technology application leverage tools and platforms to enhance efficiency, foster innovation, and achieve strategic objectives, all while aligning solutions with organizational priorities.

While technology awareness focuses on identifying relevant tools, technology application ensures that those tools are effectively integrated into day-to-day operations. Leaders must move beyond understanding emerging technologies to implementing them in ways that solve real business challenges and create competitive advantages.

The Vital Importance Of Technology Application

Technology application is critical for converting ideas into action and transforming investments into tangible outcomes. As digital tools and platforms become integral to business operations, leaders must ensure that technology serves specific, well-defined purposes rather than being adopted for its own sake. Mastering this skill allows leaders to maximize the benefits of technology while avoiding common pitfalls of misaligned or underutilized solutions.

1. Bridging Strategy and Execution

Leaders who excel in technology application integrate relevant tools effectively into the organization's operations by ensuring that investments align with strategic goals, enabling seamless implementation and meaningful outcomes.

2. Enhancing Operational Efficiency

Technology application enables organizations to optimize processes, reduce costs, and increase productivity. Leaders who translate technological capabilities into practical workflows ensure that teams can work smarter, not harder, leveraging tools to streamline operations and deliver results.

3. Driving Innovation

Leaders proficient in technology application harness digital tools to unlock new opportunities for innovation. Whether by improving customer experiences, launching new products, or creating entirely new business models, effective application of technology enables organizations to stay competitive and forward-thinking.

4. Customizing Solutions for Unique Needs

Every organization has distinct challenges and priorities. Technology application involves tailoring solutions to fit these unique contexts, ensuring that tools are fully utilized and directly address critical business needs. This customization prevents wasted resources and enhances return on investment.

With a strong emphasis on execution, technology application ensures that innovation translates into real-world impact.

Key Components Of Technology Application

To master technology application, leaders must integrate several critical components:

- *Strategic Alignment:* Ensure that technology is intentionally chosen and deployed to advance specific organizational goals, driving measurable outcomes that align with long-term strategic priorities.

- *Customization:* Adapt tools, platforms, and systems to meet the unique needs, workflows, and challenges of the organization, ensuring that technology integrates seamlessly into existing processes.

- *Collaboration:* Work closely with technical experts, end-users, and stakeholders to design, implement, and optimize solutions that are practical, user-friendly, and aligned with organizational objectives.

- *Measurement:* Track the impact of technology using clearly defined KPIs and performance metrics, regularly analyzing results to ensure that technological investments are delivering the expected benefits.

- *Iterative Improvement:* Continuously refine and enhance the application of technology, leveraging feedback and new insights to maximize value, stay competitive, and adapt to changing needs over time.

By focusing on these key components, leaders ensure that technology is not just implemented but fully integrated into the organization's strategic framework.

Familiar Examples Of Effective Technology Application

Walgreens' Digital Health Transformation

Walgreens leveraged technology to launch digital health tools, including telemedicine platforms and app-based prescription management. These applications addressed customer demands for convenience and accessibility, aligning with the company's goal of enhancing the patient experience.

Intel's Board and Strategic Use of AI

Intel's board of directors has actively guided the company's strategic investment in artificial intelligence technologies. By integrating AI into its core chip design and manufacturing processes, Intel has enhanced performance and efficiency, ensuring its products meet evolving market demands and maintain a competitive edge.

The Guardian's Digital Transition

The Guardian's leadership successfully applied technology to transition from a traditional print model to a digital-first publication. By investing in analytics, digital storytelling tools, and subscription platforms, the organization adapted to changing consumer behaviors while maintaining its journalistic integrity and mission.

These examples demonstrate how technology application drives operational efficiency, customer engagement, and competitive positioning.

Technology Application As A Repeatable Skill

Technology application is an ongoing process that evolves with advancements in tools and changing organizational needs. Leaders must stay engaged with both emerging technologies and their organization's specific challenges to ensure solutions remain aligned with strategic priorities. This continuous effort bridges the gap between technological potential and practical execution.

Collaboration is essential for successful technology application. Leaders must work closely with technical experts, frontline employees, and stakeholders to identify gaps, adapt solutions, and implement changes effectively. By fostering cross-functional partnerships, leaders ensure that technology initiatives resonate across the organization and deliver meaningful outcomes.

Finally, measuring impact is critical. Establishing clear KPIs and analyzing results allows leaders to assess whether technology investments are achieving their intended goals. This data-driven approach enables iterative improvement, ensuring that tools are refined and optimized to deliver maximum value over time.

Integrating Skills For Leadership Success

As leaders navigate today's digital landscape, it is vital to balance the mastery of professional, personal, and technology skills. Each leader's journey is shaped by unique challenges and priorities, requiring a tailored approach to growth. Intentional skill development, guided by feedback and strategic alignment, ensures that leaders remain impactful in the face of evolving organizational needs.

By understanding which competencies are most critical at any given moment, leaders can adapt to shifting market demands while staying true to long-term aspirations. In the next chapter, we'll explore practical methods for assessing and prioritizing leadership development, enabling you to craft a growth plan that reflects your strengths and aligns with your organization's goals.

Chapter Summary

This chapter explored the critical importance of technology skills for contemporary leadership, focusing on three key competencies: technology awareness, technology objectivity, and technology application. These skills enable leaders to stay informed about emerging technologies, evaluate their relevance critically, and implement them strategically to drive organizational success. The chapter emphasized how leaders must bridge the gap between innovation and strategy, leveraging technology to create value, enhance decision making, and sustain competitive advantage.

Practical examples illustrated how leaders can apply technology awareness to stay ahead of emerging trends, use technology objectivity to critically evaluate solutions without bias, and master technology application to turn possibilities into measurable outcomes. These interconnected skills enable leaders to drive digital transformation, foster innovation, and enhance organizational agility. By aligning technological advancements with strategic priorities, leaders can ensure that technology is not just adopted but leveraged effectively to create lasting value.

With the domains of Professional, Personal, and Technology Skills fully explored, the next chapter shifts focus to the assessment and development of these 15 essential skills. Chapter 6 provides a framework for evaluating leadership capabilities, identifying growth areas, and creating tailored development plans to help leaders thrive in an ever-evolving business landscape.

CHAPTER 6

ASSESSING AND DEVELOPING LEADERSHIP SKILLS: A REVISED APPROACH FOR A CHANGING WORLD

Leadership is foundational to organizational success, but the demands on today's leaders are unparalleled in complexity and urgency. Navigating the modern business landscape requires leaders to possess a portfolio of contemporary skills that go beyond traditional leadership capabilities. These include adapting to rapid technological advancements, responding to shifting workforce expectations, and tackling global and systemic challenges. The 15 contemporary leadership skills outlined in previous chapters provide a framework for leaders to meet these demands across professional, personal, and technological domains.

However, just as leadership itself must evolve, so too must the methods for assessing and developing these skills. Traditional approaches to leadership development, which often relied on generic programs or static evaluations, are no longer sufficient. Today's dynamic environment calls for a development model that is flexible, data-driven, and deeply personalized. Assessing and cultivating leadership skills must become a continuous, iterative process that evolves alongside the challenges leaders face.

This chapter introduces a simple three-step model designed to help leaders and organizations assess and develop contemporary leadership skills effectively. By moving beyond static, one-size-fits-all approaches, this model provides a dynamic framework for growth, empowering leaders to thrive in an era of constant disruption.

A Three-Step Model For Leadership Assessment And Development

Developing contemporary leadership skills requires a structured yet adaptable approach that reflects the complexity of modern business challenges. A three-step model offers a clear framework for leaders and organizations to identify current capabilities, prioritize areas for improvement, and create actionable plans for growth. While traditional models of leadership development often emphasized static competencies, this approach emphasizes flexibility, personalization, and alignment with dynamic organizational needs.

The essence of this model lies in its integration of objectivity, strategic focus, and tailored application. Leaders today face unique demands that require a more nuanced understanding of their capabilities and growth potential. By grounding development efforts in objective data, prioritizing skill gaps that align with critical goals, and crafting customized roadmaps, this model ensures that leadership development is both impactful and efficient.

At its core, the model follows three clear steps to guide leaders through the development process:

- *Step 1—Conducting an Objective Assessment*: Establishing a clear understanding of current capabilities is the foundation for effective development.

- *Step 2—Prioritizing Skill Gaps:* Identifying the most critical areas for growth ensures that resources and energy are directed where they will have the greatest impact.

- *Step 3—Designing and Implementing a Custom Leadership Development Roadmap:* Tailoring a plan to the leader's unique role and goals ensures that development efforts are actionable and aligned with broader objectives.

This structured process not only addresses immediate skill gaps but also builds a foundation for ongoing growth, enabling leaders to adapt as challenges evolve.

The Evolution Of Leadership Development

Leadership development has undergone a profound transformation in response to the growing complexity of modern organizations. Traditional models often relied on static competency frameworks, standardized training programs, and hierarchical career progression. These approaches, while effective in more stable environments, fail to meet the demands of today's fast-paced, technology-driven, and increasingly decentralized workplaces. The expectations placed on leaders have evolved beyond operational oversight and strategic execution—they must now demonstrate agility, emotional intelligence, and technological fluency to remain effective.

A major shift in leadership development has been the move from one-size-fits-all training programs to personalized, data-driven approaches. Organizations now recognize that leadership growth is not linear and must be tailored to an individual's role, industry, and career trajectory. Development initiatives are increasingly designed to be iterative, with real-time feedback loops that allow leaders to refine their skills continuously. Adaptive learning models, mentorship networks, and digital assessments now play a greater role in ensuring that leadership development is dynamic rather than static.

The three-step model introduced in this chapter reflects this shift toward customized, results-driven leadership development. By prioritizing objective assessments, targeted skill building, and individualized growth plans, this approach ensures that leaders develop the capabilities most relevant to their unique challenges. Rather than adhering to outdated frameworks, organizations must embrace leadership development as an evolving process—one that allows leaders to anticipate change, address emerging skill gaps, and drive long-term organizational success.

Why A Structured Approach Matters

The demands on contemporary leaders are higher than ever, requiring a structured yet flexible approach to skill development. Without a clear framework for growth, leadership development can become fragmented, leaving individuals and organizations uncertain about which skills to prioritize. A structured approach ensures that leadership development efforts remain intentional, measurable, and aligned with strategic goals. It provides a roadmap that helps leaders understand where they stand, what they need to improve, and how to achieve meaningful progress.

A well-defined framework also prevents leadership burnout by focusing on the most impactful areas of development. Many leaders feel overwhelmed by the expectation to excel in multiple domains—without guidance, they risk spreading themselves too thin. A structured model ensures that leadership development is prioritized, balancing short-term needs with long-term growth. This targeted focus allows leaders to address critical gaps without becoming distracted by less essential competencies, ultimately maximizing their effectiveness.

Finally, a structured approach enables organizations to measure the return on their leadership development investments. By tracking progress through objective assessments and performance metrics, organizations can ensure that leadership growth efforts translate into tangible business outcomes. A data-driven framework helps leaders refine their strategies, improve team dynamics, and contribute more effectively to organizational success. By adopting this structured yet adaptable approach, both leaders and organizations can ensure that leadership development remains impactful, sustainable, and relevant in an ever-changing world.

Step 1: Conducting An Objective Assessment Of Leadership Skills

Traditional methods of leadership assessment often fell short due to reliance on subjective evaluations, informal reviews, and a lack of actionable insights. These limitations made it challenging to accurately identify skill gaps, leaving leaders unprepared for the nuanced demands of modern business environments.

Effective leadership development begins with a comprehensive understanding of a leader's current capabilities. Without an accurate assessment, development efforts risk being misaligned, focusing on areas that do not require improvement while overlooking critical skill gaps. Objectivity is key to ensuring evaluations are accurate, actionable, and free from biases that can distort the development process.

The Importance of Objectivity in Assessments

Accurate leadership assessments depend on objectivity. Biases—whether from overly positive feedback by subordinates or critical reviews influenced by organizational politics—can distort the results. Without clear, unbiased evaluations, leaders may overlook key areas for growth or focus on skills that don't need improvement. Objective assessments provide a reliable starting point, ensuring development efforts are targeted and effective.

Modern tools play a key role in reducing subjectivity. Psychometric testing measures traits like emotional intelligence and resilience, while AI-driven analytics identify behavioral patterns in decision making and collaboration. 360-degree feedback integrates perspectives from peers, supervisors, and subordinates to provide a balanced view. These methods, when used together, uncover insights that traditional reviews may miss, such as a leader's struggle with team dynamics despite strong strategic abilities.

Objectivity also fosters trust in the development process. Leaders are more open to feedback when they know it's impartial and actionable. External experts, such as consultants or coaches, add an extra layer of neutrality, offering data-driven insights and minimizing internal bias. By prioritizing fair and accurate assessments, organizations create a solid foundation for growth and ensure leaders can focus on the skills that matter most.

Advanced Tools for Accurate Assessments

Modern tools have transformed the way leadership capabilities are assessed, offering deeper insights than traditional methods:

- *AI-driven Behavioral Analytics:* These systems analyze decision making, collaboration, and communication patterns to reveal nuanced strengths and gaps.

- *Psychometric Testing:* Tests that measure attributes such as adaptability, resilience, and emotional intelligence provide a personalized understanding of a leader's abilities.

- *360-degree Feedback Platforms:* By incorporating input from supervisors, peers, and subordinates, these platforms provide a balanced view of leadership impact.

When used together, these tools can uncover hidden strengths and blind spots. For instance, a leader who excels at strategic planning but struggles with emotional intelligence may benefit from targeted training that bridges this gap.

Practical Example: Jessica's Objective Assessment

Jessica, a regional operations manager, was well regarded for her technical problem-solving skills but struggled to foster collaboration within her team. Her organization engaged an external consultant to conduct a detailed assessment of her leadership abilities. Using psychometric tools and 360-degree feedback, the consultant identified specific gaps in Jessica's emotional intelligence and communication strategies.

With these insights, Jessica's organization was able to create a development plan tailored to her needs. This plan not only addressed her interpersonal challenges but also leveraged her existing strengths to improve team cohesion. By focusing on data-driven and unbiased evaluation, Jessica gained clarity on how to grow as a leader.

Step 2: Prioritizing Skill Gaps

Historically, leadership development often followed a generalized approach, treating all skill building as equally important. This lack of strategic prioritization often resulted in wasted effort and reduced effectiveness. In today's fast-changing world, leaders must adopt a more focused approach to development, targeting the skills that matter most for their roles and organizational contexts.

Once assessments are complete, the next step is determining where to focus development efforts. Leaders cannot effectively develop all 15 contemporary skills simultaneously. Prioritizing skill gaps ensures that resources are directed toward areas with the greatest potential to enhance leadership effectiveness and organizational success.

The Necessity of Strategic Focus

The wide range of contemporary leadership skills requires leaders to strategically focus their development efforts. Attempting to improve all skills at once can lead to overwhelm, diluted progress, and reduced effectiveness. By identifying and concentrating on a few high-priority areas, leaders can make meaningful advancements that benefit both their teams and the organization as a whole.

Strategic prioritization is not about neglecting less critical skills but about sequencing growth efforts to align with immediate demands and long-term goals. The priorities will differ significantly depending on a leader's specific role. For example, an executive who leads operations will need a vastly different skill set than a board member who focuses on governance or an entrepreneur who strives to establish a new venture. This alignment ensures that leaders remain effective within their unique contexts while preparing for future challenges.

Factors such as a leader's distinct responsibilities, organizational objectives, and personal strengths and gaps must guide prioritization. A chief technology officer (CTO) may prioritize technology awareness and decision making, while a chief human resources officer (CHRO) might focus on coaching and emotional intelligence. Meanwhile, board members may emphasize strategic visioning and stakeholder alignment, whereas entrepreneurs often prioritize resilience, adaptability, and vision translation. Tailoring development plans to these priorities ensures efforts are impactful and align with each leader's unique contributions to organizational success.

Key Considerations for Prioritization

When prioritizing skill gaps, leaders and organizations should consider three key factors:

1. Role-Specific Demands

Different leadership roles demand distinct skills. For example:

- Executives: Often responsible for operational execution and team alignment, executives may focus on decision making, problem solving, and communication. Their prioritization reflects the need to deliver short-term results while building long-term organizational capacity.

- Board Members: With a focus on governance, strategic oversight, and risk management, key skills for board members might include visioning, resilience, and the ability to align stakeholders to strategic goals.

- Entrepreneurs: In contrast, entrepreneurs need to emphasize adaptability, innovation, and translating bold visions into actionable steps. Their leadership development must prepare them to navigate uncertainty, build trust, and scale their organizations effectively.

2. Organizational Objectives

Broader goals heavily influence development priorities. For instance:

- Companies pursuing global expansion may require leaders to focus on visioning and adaptability.

- Organizations undergoing restructuring may call for leaders skilled in emotional intelligence and coaching to help navigate workforce transitions.

3. Individual Strengths And Weaknesses

A leader's current abilities and career stage should guide development efforts. For example:

- A new manager may focus on foundational skills like problem solving and communication.

- A seasoned executive may prioritize refining advanced capabilities such as resilience and decision making.

By carefully considering these factors, leaders can strategically target development efforts that align with their roles and organizational contexts. This tailored approach ensures that leadership development investments yield maximum returns.

Practical Example: Ethan's Prioritization Strategy

Ethan, the COO of a renewable energy company, faced competing priorities in his development. His operational responsibilities required strengthening decision making and delegation skills to manage day-to-day challenges effectively. Simultaneously, his long-term role as a strategic leader in sustainability called for enhanced visioning and technology awareness to drive the company's innovation agenda.

To address these needs, Ethan worked with his organization to focus on decision-making skills in the short term. He participated in leadership simulations and workshops designed to build confidence under pressure while refining delegation practices. Over time, Ethan added executive coaching sessions focused on visioning, ensuring his long-term development aligned with the company's broader sustainability objectives. This deliberate prioritization enabled Ethan to balance immediate operational demands with the future-focused leadership skills required for success.

Step 3: Designing And Implementing A Custom Leadership Development Roadmap

Leadership development plans in the past often lacked personalization, relying on standardized programs that did not account for the unique goals, roles, or challenges faced by individual leaders. Such rigid approaches are ill-suited to today's dynamic environment, where agility and alignment with organizational strategy are paramount.

The final step in the model is creating and executing a tailored roadmap for leadership growth. This roadmap provides a structured yet flexible approach to skill development, ensuring that leaders can adapt to changing circumstances while staying focused on their goals.

Building an Adaptive Development Plan

A well-designed roadmap incorporates three essential elements, with examples of how they can be customized based on context:

1. Personalized Learning Opportunities

- Workshops or training programs may help address specific skill gaps in areas like emotional intelligence or decision making.

- Experiential learning, such as cross-functional projects or stretch assignments, can give leaders real-world opportunities to apply and refine new skills.

- Mentorship programs, when feasible, provide leaders with guidance from more experienced professionals who offer insights tailored to their challenges.

2. Continuous Feedback Mechanisms

- Regular reviews, whether quarterly or on a timeline aligned with organizational needs, help monitor progress and adjust the roadmap as necessary.

- Feedback methods can include both data-driven insights (e.g., performance metrics) and qualitative approaches like one-on-one coaching or team input.

3. Alignment With Organizational Strategy

- Leaders might contribute to strategic initiatives or specific projects that reinforce their development while advancing organizational goals.

- Opportunities such as involvement in innovation efforts or workforce engagement strategies can ensure the development process has a tangible, organizational impact.

Practical Example: Tasha's Tailored Roadmap

Tasha, the founder of a tech startup, excelled in technology application but struggled with team alignment and authenticity. Her roadmap included collaborative workshops on authentic leadership, cross-functional projects to improve team cohesion, and mentorship sessions to refine her interpersonal skills.

As Tasha progressed through her plan, she noticed significant improvements in her team dynamics and overall company culture. By aligning her development efforts with both personal growth goals and organizational needs, Tasha strengthened her leadership impact and enhanced her company's performance.

Chapter Summary

Assessing and developing contemporary leadership skills requires a shift away from traditional approaches that relied on generic programs, static evaluations, and subjective feedback. These outdated methods often failed to address the unique challenges and dynamic nature of modern leadership roles. In contrast, this chapter presented a three-step model that emphasizes flexibility, data-driven insights, and personalization, offering leaders and organizations a more effective pathway to growth.

The model outlined three critical steps: conducting objective assessments, prioritizing skill gaps, and designing tailored development roadmaps. Each step reflects an evolution in leadership development, moving beyond rigid, one-size-fits-all practices to deliver targeted, actionable, and context-specific solutions. By integrating advanced tools, iterative feedback, and alignment with organizational goals, this approach equips leaders with the agility and precision required to navigate complex challenges effectively.

Practical examples throughout the chapter demonstrated how this modern model can uncover hidden strengths, address critical gaps, and empower leaders to align their growth with organizational needs. By adopting this dynamic and iterative framework, leaders can ensure their skills remain relevant and impactful in an ever-changing business environment. The next chapter delves into the consequences of neglecting leadership assessment and development, exploring how unaddressed skill gaps can disrupt organizational progress and compromise long-term resilience.

CHAPTER 7

LEADERSHIP DEFICIENCIES: THE COST OF NEGLECTING DEVELOPMENT

In previous chapters, we celebrated the transformative power of exceptional leadership. From visionary leaders who inspired groundbreaking innovation to those who built cultures of trust and adaptability, we explored how leadership excellence drives growth, resilience, and strategic success. However, great leadership is only half the story. Leadership gaps—those critical deficiencies that hinder decision making, erode trust, and derail execution—are equally vital to address. While many leadership publications shy away from discussing the consequences of poor leadership, this chapter tackles these challenges head-on. By examining how leadership deficiencies impact organizations, we underscore the urgency of adopting a modern, strategic approach to leadership development.

Leadership deficiencies are not isolated to individuals; they impact entire teams and organizations. Neglecting leadership development or allowing skill gaps to persist can derail even the most well-conceived strategies. From misaligned priorities to cultural fragmentation, leadership deficiencies amplify vulnerabilities in an increasingly volatile business environment.

This chapter examines the risks associated with leadership deficiencies and their implications for organizational outcomes. Through concise insights and practical examples, followed by detailed case studies, we reveal how deficiencies in decision making, authenticity, and adaptability disrupt execution, undermine competitive positioning, and weaken cultural cohesion. These targeted examples highlight the importance of addressing leadership gaps to strengthen impact and guide organizations toward sustainable success.

How Leadership Deficiencies Block Execution

Execution is where strategy becomes action, and leadership deficiencies create significant barriers to this process. Organic initiatives, such as launching a new product or entering a new market, depend on leaders who can effectively translate strategic goals into actionable plans. Without this ability, teams often face misaligned priorities, missed deadlines, and lost opportunities.

In more complex scenarios, such as mergers and acquisitions, execution requires additional leadership competencies, such as communication, cultural alignment, and resilience. Leaders who fail to articulate the integration process or manage expectations risk creating cultural clashes and operational inefficiencies. These gaps not only derail immediate goals but also compromise long-term value creation, leaving organizations struggling to recover.

The challenges of execution are further compounded by today's fast-paced and highly competitive landscape. Leaders who cannot adapt or pivot under pressure leave their organizations exposed to disruption and stagnation. Addressing these gaps is essential to ensuring that strategic initiatives are not only implemented effectively but also achieve their intended outcomes.

Practical Example: Linda's Misaligned Team

Linda, a product manager at a consumer electronics company, was tasked with overseeing the launch of an innovative smart home device. While the strategy for the launch was ambitious, Linda's limited translation skills created confusion among her team. Strategic goals were communicated as high-level objectives without clear actionable steps, leaving team members uncertain about priorities and deadlines.

As a result, key tasks were delayed, and the launch timeline was missed. Customer feedback revealed frustration with the product's delayed release and its lack of readiness compared to competitors' offerings. Linda's inability to translate strategy into execution derailed what could have been a market-leading product. This example highlights the importance of leaders who can break down complex strategies into clear, actionable steps to ensure successful execution.

Leadership Gaps And Competitive Positioning

Strong leadership is essential for maintaining competitive positioning in today's dynamic markets. Organic initiatives, such as product development or customer engagement strategies, require curiosity and problem-solving skills. Without these abilities, organizations struggle to identify opportunities and innovate effectively, allowing competitors to gain ground.

In inorganic efforts, such as partnerships or acquisitions, resilience is critical for navigating challenges and aligning teams. Leaders who lack adaptability may falter in the face of integration obstacles, resulting in delays or lost value. Over time, these gaps hinder an organization's ability to respond to change and maintain a competitive edge.

Leadership deficiencies ultimately erode an organization's capacity for strategic foresight. By failing to anticipate trends or prioritize innovation, organizations fall behind more agile competitors. Cultivating leadership skills such as adaptability, visioning, and problem solving is vital to ensuring sustained success.

Practical Example: Paul's Struggle with Innovation

Paul, a division head at a pharmaceutical company, faced mounting pressure to innovate in response to competition from biotech startups. Despite the organization's potential for breakthrough products, Paul resisted exploring new drug delivery methods, dismissing suggestions as too risky.

Competitors seized the opportunity to launch innovative treatments, capturing market share. Paul's hesitation not only cost the company revenue but also underscored the risks of leadership gaps in curiosity and problem solving. This example highlights how such deficiencies hinder an organization's ability to maintain its competitive position.

The Cultural Impact Of Leadership Deficiencies

Strong cultural cohesion is a cornerstone of organizational success, yet leadership deficiencies often disrupt this critical foundation. Leaders who lack emotional intelligence or coaching skills struggle to gain trust, address team concerns, and maintain morale. This erosion of engagement weakens collaboration and productivity.

Cultural fragmentation is particularly problematic during mergers or restructuring. Leaders who cannot align priorities or create a shared identity risk high turnover, disengagement, and inefficiencies. These rifts delay or derail strategic initiatives, leaving organizations struggling to regain cohesion.

Leaders with emotional intelligence and authenticity are better equipped to sustain cultural strength, even in challenging times. By fostering trust and inclusivity, they create environments where teams can thrive, driving sustained organizational performance.

Practical Example: Sara's Strained Integration

Sara, the COO of a logistics company, managed the integration of a newly acquired competitor. However, her limited emotional intelligence and coaching skills alienated acquired employees. Many felt excluded from decisions and undervalued in their roles.

The resulting disengagement led to increased turnover and missed performance targets. Sara's experience illustrates how deficiencies in emotional intelligence can disrupt cultural cohesion, undermining morale and operational success.

Lessons From Leadership Failures: Real-World Case Studies

As explored in the preceding sections, leadership deficiencies can disrupt strategic execution, weaken team dynamics, and erode an organization's ability to adapt. While practical examples are invaluable for illustrating key principles, nothing resonates more profoundly than real-world examples grounded in firsthand experience. These real scenarios not only capture the tangible consequences of leadership gaps but also offer authentic lessons drawn from actual challenges and outcomes.

The following case studies delve into situations where critical leadership deficiencies—whether in decision making, authenticity, or technology literacy—led to significant organizational setbacks. These stories, derived from the author's direct experiences (though anonymized for confidentiality), go beyond theory to reveal how leadership failures play out in practice. By studying these examples, leaders can better understand how to recognize and address similar challenges in their own contexts.

Through these detailed accounts, this chapter emphasizes the urgency of confronting leadership gaps with intentional development, ensuring leaders are equipped to navigate complexity and deliver meaningful results. Let us now examine these real-world cases and uncover their lessons.

Carter's Story: Decision Paralysis Leading To Missed Opportunities

Carter, the ambitious founder of a startup specializing in workflow management applications, had a vision to simplify complex processes for businesses. His team developed a cutting-edge app that addressed significant market pain points, offering a seamless solution for professionals seeking efficiency and ease of use. Early testing confirmed the app's potential, receiving overwhelmingly positive feedback from target users and positioning it as a likely category leader in the industry.

Despite the app's readiness for launch, Carter hesitated to release it. His perfectionist tendencies drove him to repeatedly seek additional feedback from stakeholders and refine features in pursuit of an ideal product. Months turned into over a year, and the app remained in development while competitors brought similar products to market. As competitors iterated on real-world user feedback and refined their offerings, Carter's team saw their initial advantage erode.

Carter's indecision not only delayed the app's launch but also drained company resources and morale. Team members grew frustrated with the endless cycle of revisions and the lack of tangible progress. This inability to balance preparation with timely action exposed a critical leadership deficiency: Carter's lack of decisiveness. His fear of failure and need for perfection paralyzed the startup's momentum, leaving it vulnerable to more agile competitors.

By the time Carter finally launched the app, competitors had captured significant market share and established loyal customer bases. Although the app was still innovative, its late entry into a crowded market relegated it to an afterthought. Carter's startup, once brimming with potential, struggled to recover from the missed opportunity and lost competitive positioning.

This case underscores the importance of decisive leadership in executing organic strategies like product development and market entry. Leaders must recognize that waiting for perfect conditions often results in lost opportunities. Calculated risks and timely action are not only essential to maintaining momentum but also critical for seizing competitive advantages. Carter's experience illustrates the necessity of integrating decision making with problem solving and adaptability, ensuring that organizations remain agile, competitive, and resilient in dynamic markets.

Katherine's Story: Inconsistent Leadership Stalling Strategic Alignment

Katherine, a senior executive at a consulting firm, was tasked with implementing a corporate strategy designed to enhance innovation, client outcomes, and competitive positioning. To support this ambitious initiative, the strategy was underpinned by firm-wide values that emphasized collective success over individual recognition, fostering collaboration and shared achievement. As a key leader in this effort, Katherine was expected to embody these values and inspire others to align their actions with organizational priorities.

In public, Katherine positioned herself as a vocal advocate for the strategy, delivering compelling messages about the importance of collaboration and urging employees to prioritize the firm's goals above personal achievements. Her confident and enthusiastic delivery inspired initial buy-in from employees and colleagues, positioning her as a central figure in driving alignment across the organization.

Privately, however, Katherine's actions betrayed her public rhetoric. She frequently redirected high-profile projects to her department, seeking personal recognition and visibility over advancing the collective success of the firm. This glaring inconsistency between her words and actions quickly eroded trust among her peers and subordinates. Employees began to disengage from the initiative, questioning both Katherine's sincerity and the broader commitment of senior leadership to the firm-wide values.

As skepticism spread, the strategy's momentum dissipated. Efforts to align teams across the organization faltered, collaboration weakened, and the firm failed to achieve its strategic objectives. Katherine's failure highlights the importance of authenticity—a critical leadership skill that fosters trust and alignment by ensuring consistency between a leader's words and actions. Without authenticity, even well-designed strategies risk losing credibility and support, undermining their potential for success.

This case also demonstrates how emotional intelligence and coaching skills are essential to authentic leadership. Emotional intelligence enables leaders to understand and address the concerns of their teams, fostering a culture of trust and collaboration. Coaching helps leaders guide their teams through periods of strategic change, maintaining alignment and morale. Whether driving organic innovation or managing inorganic integrations, leaders who embody these skills ensure that strategic initiatives remain credible, inspiring, and effective in achieving organizational goals.

Michael's Story: Ill-Informed Technology Decisions Producing Disastrous ROI

Michael, a seasoned board chair at a prominent financial services firm, faced the pressing challenge of navigating the organization through a period of rapid technological disruption. The financial services industry was being reshaped by advancements in AI, blockchain, and predictive analytics, offering significant opportunities for operational efficiencies and competitive differentiation. However, Michael's limited familiarity with emerging technologies left him unable to critically assess these innovations or their strategic implications.

Relying heavily on the recommendations of the firm's CTO, Michael and the board approved a series of major investments in AI-driven platforms. While the initiatives were well-intentioned, they lacked alignment with the firm's broader strategic priorities. Over the next two years, the company spent millions of dollars on poorly integrated solutions that failed to deliver measurable value. These initiatives suffered from unclear objectives, insufficient cross-departmental collaboration, and a lack of alignment with customer-centric goals.

Meanwhile, competitors in the industry approached technological adoption with precision and purpose. By focusing on targeted investments that directly supported their strategic priorities, these organizations successfully leveraged technology to streamline operations, enhance customer experiences, and strengthen their market positions. In contrast, Michael's firm struggled to justify its expenditures, and its market share eroded as competitors gained ground.

Michael's hands-off approach revealed a significant leadership gap. While board members are not required to be technologists, they must possess sufficient technology literacy to ask the right questions, evaluate proposals critically, and ensure that technological initiatives align with strategic goals. This foundational awareness enables leaders to avoid costly missteps and to leverage innovation as a strategic asset rather than an isolated project.

Michael's experience underscores the growing importance of combining technology awareness with visioning. Leaders must not only understand emerging technologies but also integrate them into a cohesive vision that aligns with organizational priorities. By failing to pair these skills, Michael approved technological initiatives that effectively operated in silos, ultimately diminishing their potential value. This case serves as a cautionary tale, highlighting that in today's fast-evolving business environment, technology literacy, even at the board level, is no longer optional—it is a critical component of effective leadership in both organic strategies, like digital transformation, and inorganic efforts, such as technology-driven partnerships.

Leadership Excellence: Redefining The Path To Success

The case studies in this chapter reveal how leadership deficiencies can derail even the most promising strategies, whether organic or inorganic.

They also illuminate a critical realization: The success of any organizational initiative ultimately hinges on leadership. Leaders are the catalysts for innovation, adaptability, and alignment, transforming vision into tangible results. Without strong leadership, traditional strategies falter under the weight of complexity and change.

As organizations navigate an increasingly volatile and interconnected world, the emphasis on leadership strategies has reached a tipping point. No longer a supporting function, leadership now stands as a core strategic driver—equally, if not more, vital than traditional growth strategies. In this new paradigm, leadership excellence becomes the foundation for sustained success, empowering organizations to thrive in the face of uncertainty.

The next chapter builds on this perspective, making the case for leadership strategies as the primary contributors to modern organizational success. By highlighting their role in driving innovation, resilience, and alignment, Chapter 8 challenges organizations to rethink their strategic priorities and embrace leadership as the most critical lever for navigating the complexities of today's business environment.

Chapter Summary

This chapter tackled the critical gaps that undermine trust, team alignment, and organizational performance. Unlike other publications that focus solely on celebrating success, we explored the costs of leadership deficiencies, such as indecision, inauthenticity, and poor adaptability. Practical examples highlighted how these gaps impact execution, competitive positioning, and cultural cohesion, while detailed case studies offered real-world lessons on the urgency of addressing these deficiencies.

Leadership deficiencies are not isolated incidents; they create vulnerabilities in a rapidly changing business environment. By cultivating skills like visioning, emotional intelligence, and resilience, leaders can mitigate these risks and drive long-term success.

Looking ahead, the next chapter explores the growing importance of leadership strategies as a critical contributor to modern organizational success. By shifting the focus to leadership development as a core driver of resilience and innovation, Chapter 8 outlines how organizations can align leadership excellence with strategic priorities, embrace leadership as the most essential lever for navigating the complexities of today's business environment, and thrive in an ever-evolving world.

CHAPTER 8

LEADERSHIP DEVELOPMENT AS THE ULTIMATE STRATEGY: MAKING THE CASE FOR LONG-TERM SUCCESS

Leadership development has historically been seen as a vital organizational function, but its role is evolving in ways that demand a fresh perspective. In a business environment defined by rapid change, increased complexity, and intense competition, leadership is no longer just a supporting mechanism—it is emerging as a primary driver of success. Traditional organic and inorganic strategies, such as market expansion, product innovation, and mergers and acquisitions, have long been viewed as the most effective pathways to achieving growth and long-term sustainability. However, the modern business landscape suggests that leadership development could very well be *the most impactful strategy for ensuring organizational resilience and success.*

As organizations navigate economic uncertainty, technological advancements, and shifting workforce expectations, the ability to cultivate and sustain strong leadership becomes increasingly crucial. Even the most well-designed strategic initiatives are vulnerable to failure without leaders who can drive execution, align teams, and foster adaptability. Leadership development not only strengthens execution capabilities but also serves as a *multiplier effect*—enhancing the impact of every other strategy within an organization. Companies that prioritize leadership development gain a competitive edge by building a culture of innovation, resilience, and continuous improvement.

This chapter explores the idea that leadership development *may be the most essential success strategy in the modern world.* While traditional strategies remain vital, their success hinges on the effectiveness of leadership. By examining leadership development's role in shaping organizational outcomes, encouraging adaptability, and driving long-term competitive advantage, this chapter makes the case that leadership development is not just an enabler of success—it is *a strategy in its own right.* Through familiar examples, we will highlight how organizations that invest in leadership development are best positioned to thrive in an era of uncertainty and complexity.

The Evolving Business Environment: The Rising Demands On Leaders

The challenges facing today's leaders are more complex and demanding than ever before. The rapid pace of technological innovation, increased globalization, and shifting workforce expectations have created an environment where traditional leadership models are no longer sufficient. Stability alone is not a sustainable leadership trait—leaders must be agile, forward-thinking, and equipped to guide their organizations through ongoing transformation. Companies that fail to cultivate leaders capable of navigating disruption risk falling behind as competitors seize opportunities created by change.

As business environments grow increasingly volatile, the expectations placed on leaders continue to rise. No longer can leaders rely solely on experience and intuition; they must now exhibit a dynamic set of competencies, including strategic decision making, emotional intelligence, and technological literacy. They must be capable of leading cross-functional, remote, and diverse teams while balancing immediate priorities with long-term vision. In today's high-stakes world, leadership excellence is not a luxury—it is a necessity for survival and sustained success. Without the ability to inspire, adapt, and drive innovation, even well-established organizations can stagnate or decline.

These growing leadership demands make development an essential investment rather than an optional initiative. Organizations must shift from viewing leadership as a static role to recognizing it as an evolving capability that requires continuous refinement. Those that commit to structured leadership development will not only be better prepared for future challenges but will also create a culture of resilience, collaboration, and growth. Leadership excellence is the ultimate differentiator in a world where change is the only constant.

Familiar Example: Airbnb—Resilience and Adaptability in a Time of Crisis

During the pandemic, Airbnb's leadership faced a near collapse of its business as global travel restrictions halted bookings. Rather than retreating, the company's leaders pivoted by focusing on long-term stays and local travel, a shift that ultimately allowed Airbnb to recover and emerge stronger. This resilience and adaptability—hallmarks of strong leadership—underscore why developing leaders who can think strategically and respond to disruption are essential in today's unpredictable business world.

Leadership Development As A Catalyst For Organic And Inorganic Success

Leadership in Organic Strategies

Organic strategies, such as product innovation, operational improvements, and geographic expansion, are fundamental to an organization's long-term success. While external market opportunities and technological advancements often create the conditions for organic growth, the ability to translate these opportunities into tangible outcomes ultimately depends on leadership. Without skilled leaders to drive execution, even the most promising growth strategies can falter due to slow decision making, misaligned priorities, or an inability to adapt to shifting conditions. Leadership excellence ensures that organic growth efforts remain focused, strategic, and responsive to market dynamics.

Organizations that embed leadership development into their organic strategies foster a culture of agility, problem solving, and innovation. Leaders who cultivate adaptability, curiosity, and resilience are better equipped to inspire teams, encourage experimentation, and manage complexity. By developing leaders who can translate high-level strategy into day-to-day execution, organizations ensure that their innovation pipelines remain strong, operational improvements are sustained, and market expansion efforts are seamlessly executed. Leadership at all levels—executive, managerial, and frontline—plays a crucial role in maintaining momentum and overcoming roadblocks that arise during organic growth initiatives.

Investing in leadership development as part of an organization's organic strategy also creates long-term competitive advantages. Companies with leaders who can anticipate change, empower employees, and align execution with strategic objectives are more likely to sustain growth over time. Leadership is not just about directing strategy—it is about creating the conditions for success. Organizations that recognize this reality and prioritize leadership development will be best positioned to seize opportunities and navigate challenges, ensuring that their organic growth strategies deliver measurable and lasting impact.

Familiar Example: Zoom—Agile Leadership Driving Explosive Growth

Zoom's rapid rise during the pandemic was not solely due to market demand—it was driven by leadership that prioritized agility, customer needs, and operational excellence. The company's ability to scale its

infrastructure, enhance security, and maintain user trust was a direct result of leadership decisions that aligned with its organic growth strategy.

Leadership in Inorganic Strategies

Inorganic strategies, such as mergers, acquisitions, and strategic partnerships, require a distinct set of leadership capabilities. While financial
modeling, due diligence, and operational synergies are critical to identifying and structuring deals, the success of these initiatives often hinges
on the ability of leaders to navigate complexity and guide organizations
through periods of significant change. Without skilled leadership, inorganic strategies frequently fall victim to cultural misalignment, unclear
communication, or resistance to change, leading to underperformance
or outright failure. Leadership deficiencies in this context can derail
even the most promising integrations.

Organizations that prioritize leadership development in the execution of inorganic strategies position themselves for greater success.
Leaders who possess emotional intelligence, coaching skills, and cultural awareness are better equipped to manage the human dynamics of
integration, ensuring that employees from merging entities feel valued
and aligned with shared goals. These leaders can bridge cultural divides,
address concerns proactively, and foster collaboration, minimizing disruptions while maximizing the synergies that partnerships or acquisitions are designed to achieve. Effective leadership transforms potentially
contentious transitions into opportunities for unification and growth.

Leadership development also enables organizations to address the
long-term challenges of sustaining the value created through inorganic
strategies. Leaders who can articulate a clear vision, build trust, and
maintain alignment ensure that strategic objectives are met well beyond
the initial integration phase. By embedding leadership excellence into
the DNA of inorganic efforts, organizations not only mitigate risks but
also unlock new opportunities for innovation, operational efficiency,

and market expansion. In this way, leadership becomes the connective tissue that transforms financial and operational strategies into meaningful, sustained success.

Familiar Example: Amazon and Whole Foods—Leadership Alignment in Strategic Integration

Amazon's acquisition of Whole Foods demonstrated the power of leadership alignment in an inorganic strategy. By integrating Whole Foods' brand identity with Amazon's logistics and digital ecosystem, the company leveraged leadership-driven decision making to maximize operational efficiencies and enhance customer value.

Leadership Development As A Competitive Advantage

Organizations that prioritize leadership development as a strategic imperative consistently achieve superior results, outpacing competitors in areas like innovation, agility, and employee engagement. A robust leadership pipeline enables organizations to cultivate a high-performance culture where talent thrives, creativity flourishes, and teams remain deeply aligned with strategic objectives. Leadership development also enhances an organization's ability to attract and retain top-tier talent as it signals a commitment to employee growth and advancement. In a fast-changing and competitive landscape, companies that embed leadership development into their core strategies gain a significant edge in maintaining relevance and driving success.

Leadership development is particularly critical for fostering resilience at all levels of an organization. In today's unpredictable business environment, where market disruptions and global crises have become the norm, leaders must possess the ability to navigate uncertainty and manage change effectively. By equipping leaders with the skills to pivot strategies, make decisive choices, and sustain organizational stability, leadership development ensures that companies are not merely reactive but proactive in shaping their futures. Resilient leaders can inspire confidence, maintain morale, and align teams, even during the most challenging periods.

Beyond immediate benefits, leadership development positions organizations for long-term success by embedding adaptability, emotional intelligence, and innovation into their leadership culture. Companies that invest in developing their leaders build a foundation for sustained excellence, creating a ripple effect that strengthens organizational cohesion and operational execution. By leveraging leadership development as a strategic differentiator, organizations ensure they are prepared to meet the demands of today's challenges while remaining agile enough to capitalize on tomorrow's opportunities.

Familiar Example: LinkedIn—Leadership Development Driving Engagement and Innovation

LinkedIn's leadership-centric culture is a prime example of how leadership development translates into a competitive advantage. By prioritizing mentorship, coaching, and employee growth, LinkedIn has built an engaged workforce that continues to propel the company's innovation and success.

Is Leadership Development The Ultimate Success Strategy?

While traditional growth strategies such as product innovation, market acquisitions, and technological advancements remain essential, their success hinges on the quality of leadership guiding their execution. Leadership excellence is the factor that transforms high-level strategies into actionable outcomes, ensuring initiatives are not only implemented effectively but sustained over the long term. Without capable leaders at the helm, even the most well-conceived plans risk stagnation, misalignment, or outright failure. Leadership development, therefore, serves as the unifying element that enables organizations to bridge the gap between strategy and execution.

What sets leadership development apart as a potentially ultimate success strategy is its scalability and universal applicability. Unlike industry-specific approaches that may become obsolete with economic fluctuations or technological disruptions, leadership development addresses a core human element that remains relevant across all industries and organizational models. Strong leadership enables organizations to adapt to shifting landscapes, maintain alignment through change, and drive innovation in a way that transcends temporary market trends. By embedding leadership development into their strategic priorities, organizations can create a foundation for enduring success that weathers external pressures and positions them as resilient market leaders.

The enduring power of leadership development lies in its ability to unlock potential at every level of the organization. By equipping leaders with essential skills like emotional intelligence, adaptability, and strategic vision, organizations foster a culture that thrives on collaboration, resilience, and innovation. This approach not only ensures short-term success but also establishes a legacy of growth and impact that sets the stage for long-term excellence. While traditional strategies remain vital, leadership development emerges as a transformative force, empowering organizations to navigate complexity and secure their place in an increasingly dynamic world.

Familiar Example: Adobe—Leadership-driven Innovation and Strategic Adaptability

Adobe's transformation from a software company into a leader in digital media and marketing was fueled by leadership-driven innovation. By fostering a culture of continuous leadership development, Adobe ensured its ability to pivot, grow, and remain a dominant force in its industry.

Chapter Summary

This chapter explored leadership development as *a potentially unparalleled success strategy*, one that amplifies traditional growth strategies and serves as a primary driver of resilience, adaptability, and execution. By examining the evolving demands on leaders and the role of leadership development in organic and inorganic strategies, we demonstrated how organizations that prioritize leadership excellence create sustainable competitive advantages. Familiar examples reinforced how companies that develop strong leaders are more adept at responding to uncertainty, aligning teams, and driving long-term innovation.

While traditional strategies remain valuable, leadership development is the *multiplier effect* that enhances their effectiveness. Organizations that invest in building a leadership culture unlock their full potential by ensuring that every strategic decision is supported by capable, forward-thinking leaders. By treating leadership development as a strategic imperative rather than a supplemental initiative, businesses position themselves for sustained success in an increasingly complex and competitive world.

As the final chapter of the book's core content, this discussion ties together the key concepts introduced earlier: the evolving demands on leaders, the framework of the 15 essential skills, and the imperative for leadership development to remain central to organizational strategy. The responsibility now shifts to readers to take these lessons forward, rethinking their approach to leadership and embracing their roles as catalysts for transformation, growth, and success. Whether leading a team, shaping an organization, or influencing an industry, the leaders who commit to continuous development will be the ones who define the future.

CONCLUSION

A MODERN CLIMATE DEMANDS MODERN LEADERS

The demands of the contemporary business landscape have reshaped the very fabric of leadership. Rapid advancements in technology, the globalization of markets, and the growing need for cultural sensitivity and emotional intelligence have created a climate where traditional leadership approaches are no longer sufficient. Leaders today must not only adapt to these evolving demands but actively position themselves to thrive. This requires expanding skill sets, embracing innovation, and responding to change with agility and purpose.

Throughout this book, we've seen how organizations achieve remarkable transformations when their leaders adopt modern strategies and skills. Examples like logistics companies leveraging AI to optimize supply chains or retail chains revitalizing employee engagement through coaching models demonstrate how impactful contemporary leadership can be. Success today depends not solely on operational expertise or technical know-how but on a leader's ability to balance strategic clarity with empathy, technological awareness with adaptability, and personal authenticity with professional acumen. Leadership today is an exercise in equilibrium—mastering these intersections is what sets great leaders apart.

This evolving leadership climate also presents unparalleled opportunities for those ready to rise. It is a call to action for leaders to become proactive architects of the future rather than passive observers of change. Embracing this call means cultivating a mindset of continuous learning, exploring innovative solutions, and fostering diverse teams that reflect the complexity of today's world. Leaders who meet this challenge are not merely navigating the future—they are shaping it. Modern challenges demand modern leaders equipped not only to respond to change but to define its trajectory.

Focus On Developing The Skills That Best Align With Your Mandate

As outlined in this book, contemporary leaders must navigate a complex and rapidly evolving landscape by mastering 15 essential skills across professional, personal, and technology domains. However, no leader can excel in all these areas simultaneously. The key to impactful leadership lies in identifying and prioritizing the skills that best align with your specific mandate, organizational needs, and personal strengths. By tailoring your development efforts, you can focus on what matters most for your role, ensuring that your growth directly supports the objectives you are tasked with achieving.

The 15 skills identified in this book provide a comprehensive framework, but their immediate relevance depends on the unique challenges and opportunities you face. For instance, a leader focused on digital transformation might prioritize technology literacy and adaptability, while someone overseeing a cultural change initiative could emphasize emotional intelligence and coaching. By strategically selecting which skills to develop, leaders can align their growth with both organizational goals and market realities, amplifying their impact.

Effective skill development is not just about addressing current challenges but about positioning yourself for future opportunities. By leveraging the 15 essential skills as a roadmap, you can strategically enhance your capabilities in areas that align with your long-term vision. Leadership is a dynamic and evolving journey, and by prioritizing the skills most relevant to your mandate, you ensure that your development remains purposeful and aligned with both immediate demands and broader goals.

Embrace The Opportunity To Distinguish Yourself

Leadership today is defined by complexity, disruption, and relentless change. The leaders who rise to the occasion—those who deliberately assess their capabilities, develop contemporary skills, and embrace adaptability—are the ones who will not only survive but thrive. The 15 contemporary leadership skills outlined in this book provide a roadmap for those who seek to lead with impact, whether navigating organizational challenges, driving technological innovation, or inspiring their teams through uncertainty.

Consider the example of Ethan, the COO of a renewable energy company, whose leadership journey reflects the necessity of continuous assessment and development. Ethan faced competing priorities: managing operational efficiency while positioning his company at the forefront of sustainable innovation. By systematically evaluating his leadership strengths and gaps, he identified decision making and delegation as immediate areas for growth, while long-term visioning and technology awareness became future priorities. Through a structured approach to leadership development, Ethan refined his ability to balance operational demands with strategic foresight, ultimately strengthening both his leadership effectiveness and his organization's competitive edge.

Ethan's journey underscores the power of intentional skill development. Leadership is not static—it requires ongoing self-reflection, a commitment to growth, and the willingness to challenge assumptions. Those who actively refine their leadership capabilities set themselves apart in an era where organizations desperately need forward-thinking, resilient leaders. The opportunity to distinguish yourself is in your hands. By embracing contemporary leadership skills and a structured approach to development, you are not only preparing for the challenges ahead—you are shaping the future of leadership itself.

Leadership Excellence May Be Your True Secret To Success

Leadership development extends far beyond personal growth—it is a strategic imperative that drives organizational innovation, cultural transformation, and long-term success. While traditional strategies like organic growth (focusing on internal development and market expansion) and inorganic growth (through acquisitions and partnerships) remain critical, investments in leadership development often yield more impactful and sustainable results. After all, strong leadership is the engine that powers every other strategy, ensuring their successful execution and amplifying their impact across the organization.

Consider the healthcare provider that integrated a smaller competitor with remarkable success. While the inorganic strategy of acquisition provided a pathway to expansion, it was the leadership team's focus on emotional intelligence and clear communication that enabled seamless cultural integration, reduced turnover, and enhanced overall outcomes. Without this emphasis on leadership excellence, the merger could have resulted in misalignment, disengaged employees, and lost opportunities. This example illustrates that even the most well-conceived growth strategies depend on the quality of leadership to translate potential into performance.

Leadership excellence is also unique in its ability to build resilience and foster innovation—two critical assets in today's volatile business environment. Leaders who inspire collaboration, embrace technology, and motivate teams create a competitive edge that cannot be easily replicated. Unlike organic or inorganic strategies, which can be matched or outpaced by competitors, the impact of leadership development is enduring and transformative. It aligns and galvanizes the entire organization, ensuring that all other growth initiatives are executed with precision and adaptability. Investing in leadership development is not merely a complement to other strategies; it is often the foundational driver of organizational success.

Expanding The Conversation: What Comes Next

Leadership development is not a one-size-fits-all journey. While this book has explored the critical skills required for contemporary leadership, the application of these principles varies significantly based on a leader's unique role and responsibilities. Board members face governance-level challenges that demand strategic foresight and big-picture thinking. Executives must navigate the complexities of operational execution and corporate strategy. Entrepreneurs operate in fast-paced, resource-constrained environments where adaptability and innovation are paramount.

This book serves as the foundation for a broader conversation about leadership excellence, one that adapts to the needs of those shaping governance, strategy, and entrepreneurial innovation. Future explorations may focus on the distinct leadership imperatives within these stakeholder groups, providing tailored insights to address their specific challenges.

If the insights in this book have resonated with you, I encourage you to reflect on how these principles align with your unique role. The skills discussed here form a universal framework, but their application must be tailored to your environment. Whether you are a board member defining organizational direction, an executive charged with implementing strategies, or an entrepreneur forging new paths, the leadership journey remains the ultimate differentiator.

Stay engaged, continue to develop your leadership capabilities, and recognize that this journey is ongoing. As we expand this conversation in the future, the goal will remain the same: empowering leaders at all levels to embrace adaptability, foresight, and innovation to drive meaningful impact.

Reiterating A Call To Action

The call to action presented at the outset of *The Contemporary Leader* resonates even more powerfully as this book concludes. The modern business environment is not static—it is constantly evolving, demanding leaders who can not only keep pace with change but also drive it. The journey to becoming a contemporary leader is not optional; it is essential for those who aspire to lead with purpose, vision, and impact.

Whether you lead at the governance level, in corporate strategy, or as an entrepreneur, the foundational skills outlined in this book provide the tools you need to thrive in your unique leadership role. Reflect on the transformational examples shared in these chapters. Logistics companies that leveraged AI to revolutionize supply chains and retail organizations that revitalized employee engagement through coaching are not merely practical examples; they are blueprints for what is possible when leadership becomes a priority. These stories illustrate how leaders who embrace adaptability, foresight, and innovation can create extraordinary outcomes for their teams and organizations.

Your leadership journey begins with a commitment to growth and evolution. This means enhancing emotional intelligence to deepen connections, refining visioning skills to create a strategic path forward, and integrating technological literacy into your leadership toolkit. Each step you take reinforces your ability to lead with authenticity, inspire confidence, and foster innovation.

The world is waiting for leaders who are ready to shape the future—not just adapt to it. The question is not whether you should evolve, but how quickly and decisively you will embrace this opportunity. As you close this book, let it serve as a reminder that the time to lead is now. Take action, invest in your development, and step boldly into the role of a transformative leader. The future is yours to define.

ABOUT THE AUTHOR

For over three decades, Tom Mawhinney has navigated the ever-evolving business landscape as a board member, senior executive, consultant, and entrepreneur. His career has spanned industries, continents, and economic cycles—each experience reinforcing a fundamental truth: leadership is the catalyst for organizational success.

A recognized expert in contemporary leadership, strategic growth, and emerging technologies, Tom has helped businesses worldwide evolve, adapt, and thrive in an era of rapid transformation. His ability to bridge the gap between traditional leadership principles and the disruptive forces of AI, digital transformation, and shifting workforce dynamics has made him a sought-after advisor to executives and board members alike.

Driven by an insatiable curiosity and a commitment to continuous learning, Tom remains at the forefront of leadership evolution. His thought leadership, built on years of hands-on experience and keen market insight, offers a pragmatic approach to navigating the complexities of modern business. In his writing, speaking, and advisory roles, he empowers leaders to embrace change, unlock potential, and drive sustained growth in an unpredictable world.

Email: Tom@TheContemporaryLeader.com
Website: www.TheContemporaryLeader.com
LinkedIn: https://www.linkedin.com/in/tommawhinney

THE CONTEMPORARY LEADER SERIES

The Contemporary Leader Series is a modern leadership collection designed for today's rapidly evolving business landscape. Based on the foundational framework introduced in The Contemporary Leader, each book delivers role-specific insights tailored to the unique demands of board members, executives, and entrepreneurs.

Whether you're guiding strategy from the boardroom, driving performance as a senior executive, or building the future as a founder, this series helps you translate essential leadership skills into practical impact. With a focus on professional, personal, and technology domains, each volume equips you to lead with agility, foresight, and purpose in an era of constant change.

The Contemporary Leader

The foundational leadership guide for navigating today's fast-changing business environment across all leadership contexts.

The Contemporary Board Member

A practical approach to governing with strategic clarity, long-range insight, and confidence in complexity.

The Contemporary Executive

Equipping operational leaders with the skills to lead teams, drive results, and adapt to ongoing transformation.

The Contemporary Entrepreneur

Designed for builders and founders scaling with speed, purpose, and modern leadership capability.

DID YOU ENJOY THIS BOOK?

If you enjoyed reading this book, you can help by suggesting it to someone else you think might like it, and **please leave a positive review** wherever you purchased it. This does a lot in helping others find the book. We thank you in advance for taking a few moments to do this.

THANK YOU

You might also like other Thin Leaf Press titles:

The AI Mindset: Thriving Within Civilization's Next Big Disruption

Peak Performance: Mindset Tools for Managers

Peak Performance: Mindset Tools for Sales

Peak Performance: Mindset Tools for Leaders

Peak Performance: Mindset Tools for Business

Peak Performance: Mindset Tools for Entrepreneurs

Peak Performance: Mindset Tools for Athletes

The Successful Mind: Tools to Living a Purposeful, Productive, and Happy Life

The Successful Body: Using Fitness, Nutrition, and Mindset to Live Better

The Successful Spirit: Top Performers Share Secrets to a Winning Mindset

Winning Mindset: Elite Strategies for Peak Performance

Winner's Mindset: Peak Performance Strategies for Success

The Life Coach's Tool Kit, Vol. 1

The Life Coach's Tool Kit, Vol. 2

The Life Coach's Tool Kit, Vol. 3

Ordinary to Extraordinary

The Magical Lightness of Being

Explore.

www.ingramcontent.com/pod-product-compliance
Lightning Source LLC
Chambersburg PA
CBHW051314120626
46547CB00015B/2238